PASTA
NIGHT

KATE McMILLAN

PHOTOGRAPHS BY ERIN KUNKEL

weldon**owen**

CONTENTS

 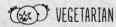

PASTA FOR DINNER

Versatile, family-friendly, and delicious—pasta has everything going for it. Plus, because pasta dishes seldom call for more than a handful of ingredients, a sauté pan, and a pot of boiling water, they move quickly and easily from the stove top to the table, making them the perfect choice for cooks with busy lives.

Pasta is the ideal dish for a family weeknight supper or a Saturday dinner for company. It can be a light tangle of tagliatelle tossed with just a vegetable or two and a scattering of herbs or a hearty plate of pappardelle dressed with a slowly simmered pork ragù. It can even be prepared in advance: assemble a baked pasta a day or even weeks ahead, refrigerate or freeze it, and then slip it into the oven to bake just before your guests arrive.

In these pages, you'll find dozens of appealing recipes, a wealth of valuable tips, and inspired ideas for putting together meals with pasta at the center. There are recipes for vegetarian, meat, and seafood pastas, for baked pastas, and for low-fat and dairy-free pastas. For a casual family dinner, you might serve spaghetti and meatballs. When guests are at the table, it is easy to introduce such special ingredients as fresh salmon, creamy burrata cheese, or homemade bread crumbs. You can even make most recipes gluten-free by using dried pasta made from brown rice, corn, or quinoa instead of wheat. You'll also find a carefully assembled selection of sides and salads to complement whichever pasta you choose.

Finally, pasta night is all about variety. A broad range of sauces—light and lean, rich and cheesy, tomatoey, creamy, meaty, vegetarian—can be matched with an equally wide array of pasta shapes and sizes—thin strands, ribbons, tubes, short and curved, short and straight, ridged and smooth—so you'll never run out of ideas for dinner. In other words, there is a dish to satisfy every pasta lover, young or old, finicky or easygoing, traditional or modern. But perhaps the best part of pasta night is how quickly and easily the meal comes together, leaving both the cook and the diners more time at the table.

ANATOMY OF A PASTA DISH

A pasta dish is made up of two basic components, the pasta and the sauce, which must be thoughtfully chosen to complement each other. Use these tips to help select the perfect marriage of pasta and sauce and some ideas for topping the finished dish.

PASTA

All pastas can be divided into two basic types, dried and fresh. One is not better than the other, but rather each has its own role in the pasta repertoire. Dried pasta has a chewy, hardy texture with a slightly rough surface, while fresh pasta is soft, silky, and moist. Keep packages of your favorite dried pasta shapes on hand for a quick meal. Because fresh pasta is perishable, purchase it or make it no more than a day in advance of serving.

SAUCE

Sauces can be heavy or delicate, fluid or chunky, rustic or refined. A rich sauce, such as a cream-based Alfredo, should just barely coat the pasta, while a tomato-based sauce, such as *amatriciana*, can be applied more generously.

TOPPINGS

A dusting of grated Parmesan cheese, a drizzle of extra-virgin olive oil, a sprinkle of flaked sea salt or red pepper flakes, a scattering of buttery bread crumbs or chopped herbs—each of these toppings can heighten the flavors of a pasta dish and elevate the final result.

PAIRING PASTAS & SAUCES

Different dried pasta shapes—smooth or ridged, long or short, thick or thin—capture and absorb sauces differently. For example, the craters and curves of the larger shapes, such as fusilli, rigatoni, or ziti, are designed to trap chunky, rustic sauces, while small shapes, like pennette, typically marry well with smooth sauces, such as pesto. Long, thin strands also mate well with fluid mixtures, while ribbons, such as fettuccine, can handle a heavier sauce. Delicate and porous fresh pasta is ideally matched with rich sauces made from butter or cream.

When pairing a pasta shape and a sauce, always keep this basic tip in mind: large pieces of protein or vegetable pair better with large pasta shapes, such as rigatoni or ziti, while thinly sliced, more tender foods, like asparagus or mushrooms, are better suited to a thin strand or ribbon pasta, such as spaghetti or tagliatelle.

PASTA PRIMER

Making a pasta dinner any night of the week is quick and easy with just a few common kitchen tools (see right), a little prep work, and some everyday kitchen skills. Here are some guidelines to guarantee success every time.

STOCK YOUR INGREDIENTS Always keep an array of basic ingredients—dried pastas, olive oil, olives, capers, anchovies, artichoke hearts, onions, garlic—in the pantry or refrigerator. If time permits, make a trip to your local farmers' market or Italian deli to pick up a few special ingredients, such as a wedge of Italian-imported Parmesan cheese, seasonal fresh vegetables and herbs, or fresh pasta.

MATCH YOUR PASTA & SAUCE Review Pairing Pastas and Sauces on page 8 to make sure your pasta and sauce will complement each other.

PLAN AHEAD Set out everything you'll need for the recipe—tools and ingredients—before you start cooking, then prep any ingredients and put the water on to boil. Never add the pasta to the boiling water until you are sure the sauce and any toppings are ready or nearly ready for serving. That way you won't end up with cooked pasta that has sat too long and clumped together.

SEASON FROM THE INSIDE To ensure a well-seasoned pasta dish, salt the pasta cooking water until it is almost as salty as seawater. Always use plenty of water (5–6 qt/5–6 l for every 1 lb/500 g of pasta) and make sure it is at a full rolling boil before you add the pasta.

ACHIEVE AL DENTE PERFECTION Pasta is best cooked al dente, literally "to the tooth" in Italian, which means the pasta noodle or shape should be tender but still firm to the bite. If using dried pasta, follow the package instructions, then sample a piece 1–2 minutes before the suggested cooking time is reached. If using fresh pasta, cook for the minimum amount of time indicated in the recipe, then sample a piece.

SAVE SOME COOKING WATER Before draining the pasta, reserve about 1 cup (8 fl oz/ 250 ml) of the cooking water in a measuring pitcher or bowl. This starchy water can be used later to help adjust the consistency of the sauce.

USE CHEESE LIGHTLY AT FIRST Have cheese at room temperature before adding it to a pasta dish, to ensure it blends in easily and does not cool down the pasta. Add just a touch of grated cheese to begin with, then pass additional cheese at the table. If grating the cheese yourself, wait until just before serving, for maximum freshness.

THE RIGHT TOOLS FOR THE JOB

LARGE POT Choose a tall, narrow pot large enough to accommodate 5–6 qt (5–6 l) water comfortably, with plenty of room for the pasta to cook at a rolling boil without sticking together.

LARGE COLANDER Look for a sturdy colander with feet, so it can be placed in the sink for hands-free draining.

METAL TONGS & WOODEN SPOON Both tools are ideal for stirring and serving pasta. Tongs work best for dishes featuring long noodles, such as spaghetti, while a long-handled wooden spoon is handy for stirring sauces and serving short noodles or pasta shapes.

BAKING DISH An ovenproof dish that is also beautiful is a one-pot solution for baked pastas. Don't forget to protect your dining table from the heat of the dish with a trivet.

CHEESE GRATER A box grater, which allows you to grate and shred cheeses into a variety of different consistencies, is great for kitchen use. A handheld grater is nice to have when you want to pass around a wedge of cheese for grating at the table.

BRINGING IT ALL TOGETHER

Having the ingredients prepped and ready to go will ensure your meal comes together smoothly. Before beginning on the sauce, measure all of the ingredients. When you're ready to assemble the pasta, have the cheese grated, the sauce and topping ready, and any necessary tools nearby.

FREEZER TIPS

SAUCES Make a large batch of one or more go-to sauces and freeze in 2–4-serving portions in freezer-safe containers. The night before serving, move the frozen container to the fridge to thaw.

SAUCE COMPONENTS Many favorite components, from meatballs to roasted vegetables, can be cooked, cooled, and frozen in freezer-safe containers.

FRESH HERBS Fresh herbs, which can wilt quickly, can be preserved in the freezer. Remove the stems, chop the leaves, and place a tablespoon of the chopped herbs in the bottom of each compartment of a clean ice-cube tray. Top off the compartments with olive oil and place in the freezer. Before using, unmold the cubes and thaw in the fridge.

BAKED DISHES Most baked pasta dishes can be fully prepared, then frozen. Complete all the steps up to the final baking instructions, then cover tightly and store in the freezer. The night before serving, move the dish to the fridge to thaw, then follow the baking directions.

SHORTCUTS FOR A BUSY DAY

Many pasta dishes are quick and easy to assemble, but here are some shortcuts to help get dinner on the table when time is limited and everybody is hungry.

SAUCES Purchase jarred or canned sauces for easy assembly. For the best fresh flavor, look for pestos and other specialty sauces at deli counters and gourmet food stores.

CHEESE & TOPPINGS You can save prep time by purchasing already-prepared items, such as preshredded cheeses, sliced prosciutto and other cured meats, pitted olives, and roasted vegetables.

SIDES & SALADS A few handfuls of fresh salad greens, such as arugula, spinach, or baby kale, dressed in olive oil and lemon juice or vinegar make an easy side salad. Or, pick up a favorite premade salad or side dish from the prepared-foods section of your grocery store.

WEEKEND PASTA PARTY

The weekend is a perfect time to invite friends for a family-friendly pasta feast. A make-your-own pasta buffet allows guests to get creative with their pasta dish. Here are some tips:

PREP THE TOPPINGS IN ADVANCE A variety of protein choices, chopped vegetables, and other savory offerings, such as olives and fresh herbs, will ensure plenty of options for guests. Items like meatballs and roasted vegetables can be made a day or two ahead of time and refrigerated.

MAKE 1–3 SAUCES IN ADVANCE Bolognese (page 20) and Pesto (page 21) are classic crowd-pleasers. To gauge how much sauce to make, figure on about ¼ cup (2 fl oz/60 ml) for each guest.

CREATE A PASTA BUFFET Start with plates and utensils, then leave space for bowls of pasta; next, place sauces and ladles for serving, followed by additional ingredients or toppings, such as red pepper flakes, flaked sea salt, and grated cheeses.

BOIL THE WATER Before your guests arrive, bring a large pot of generously salted water to a rolling boil. Add the pasta just a few minutes before you plan to eat. Then, drain the pasta, toss it with a light coating of olive oil, and add it to the buffet line, along with tongs for serving.

MAKE IT A MEAL Ask guests to bring their favorite side dish or salad for a balanced feast.

SAUCES

WHAT YOU NEED

---

2 tablespoons olive oil

1 small yellow onion, finely chopped

3 cloves garlic, minced

1 can (28 oz/875 g) crushed tomatoes

Kosher salt and freshly ground pepper

½ teaspoon dried oregano

MARINARA SAUCE

ARRABBIATA SAUCE

>>>>>>>>>

To turn this staple sauce into Arrabbiata Sauce—a red sauce with a spicy kick (arrabbiata literally means angry in Italian)—add ½ teaspoon red pepper flakes, or more if you like heat, along with the garlic.

Warm the olive oil in a heavy-bottomed, nonreactive saucepan over medium heat. Add the onion and sauté until translucent, about 5 minutes. Add the garlic and sauté just until soft, about 1 minute longer.

Stir in the tomatoes with their juice and season with salt and pepper. Raise the heat to medium-high and bring to a boil. Reduce the heat to low, add the oregano, and simmer for 15 minutes. Remove from the heat. Taste and adjust the seasoning.

Use right away, or let the sauce cool completely before storing in an airtight container in the refrigerator for up to 2 weeks or in the freezer for up to 2 months.

MAKES ABOUT 3 CUPS (24 FL OZ/750 ML)

2 tablespoons olive oil

4 oz (125 g) guanciale, pancetta,
or unsmoked bacon, chopped

1 small yellow onion, chopped

½ teaspoon crushed red pepper flakes

3 cloves garlic, minced

Kosher salt and freshly ground pepper

1 can (28 oz/875 g) crushed tomatoes

½ teaspoon dried oregano

AMATRICIANA SAUCE

Warm the oil in a saucepan, and add the guanciale. Cook the meat until it is crispy, stirring occasionally, about 5 minutes and then add the onion. Add the onion and sauté until translucent, about 5 minutes. Add the crushed red pepper flakes, the garlic, season with salt and pepper, and cook until garlic softens, 1–2 minutes. Stir in the tomatoes with their juice and bring to a boil. Reduce heat to low, add the oregano, and simmer for 15 minutes. Season with salt and pepper.

Use right away, or let the sauce cool completely before storing in an airtight container in the refrigerator for up to 1 week or in the freezer for up to 2 months.

MAKES ABOUT 3 CUPS (24 FL OZ/750 ML)

MAKE IT MEATY

This spicy version of marinara sauce has a distinct flavor with the addition of guanciale and crushed red pepper flakes. Guanciale is cured pork cheek and can be found in the butcher's section of grocery stores. The small amount of guanciale lends a meaty accent to the sauce.

2 tablespoons olive oil

4 cloves garlic, chopped

12 oil-packed anchovies, drained

½ teaspoon red pepper flakes

1 can (28 oz/875 g) diced tomatoes

½ cup (3 oz/90 g) Kalamata olives, pitted and sliced in half lengthwise

3 tablespoons capers, drained

Freshly ground pepper

PUTTANESCA SAUCE

Warm the olive oil in a heavy-bottomed, nonreactive saucepan over medium heat. Add the garlic, anchovies, and red pepper flakes and cook, stirring often, until the anchovies dissolve, about 3 minutes.

Add the tomatoes with their juice, olives, and capers along with 4 or 5 grinds of fresh pepper. Raise the heat to medium-high and bring to a boil, then reduce the heat to low and simmer for 10 minutes. Remove from the heat. Taste and adjust the seasoning.

Use right away, or let the sauce cool completely before storing in an airtight container in the refrigerator for up to 3 days. Do not freeze.

MAKES ABOUT 3 CUPS (24 FL OZ/750 ML)

A SAUCE THAT PACKS A PUNCH

This classic sauce is so flavorful, just toss it with pasta and call it a meal. Be sure to taste the sauce before you season it—the anchovies, capers, and olives already contribute a lot of saltiness.

2 tablespoons olive oil

1 carrot, peeled and cut into small dice

1 rib celery, cut into small dice

½ yellow onion, cut into small dice

Kosher salt and freshly ground pepper

3 cloves garlic, chopped

½ lb (250 g) *each* ground beef and veal

2 oz (60 g) pancetta, cut into small dice

½ cup (4 fl oz/125 ml) dry red wine

3 tablespoons tomato paste

2–3 cups (16–24 fl oz/500–750 m) low-sodium beef broth

BOLOGNESE SAUCE

A VERSATILE CLASSIC

This rustic, meaty sauce originated in Bologna, Italy, hence it's name, and is delicious served over broad and long pasta noodles like tagliatelle and fettuccine. You can also use this sauce in lasagna and other baked dishes to create a hearty crowd-friendly dish. A traditional bolognese calls for beef, veal, and pancetta but you can substitute just about any meat you want with great results.

Warm the olive oil in a heavy-bottomed, nonreactive saucepan over medium-high heat. Add the carrot, celery, and onion and season with salt and pepper. Sauté until the vegetables are soft, about 7 minutes. Add the garlic and sauté just until soft, about 1 minute longer.

Add the beef, veal, and pancetta, season with salt and pepper, and cook, stirring often, using your spoon to break up any clumps, until the meat is browned, about 10 minutes. Add the wine and cook until the liquid is reduced by about half, about 4 minutes.

Stir in the tomato paste and 2 cups (16 fl oz/500 ml) of the beef broth and season again with salt and pepper. Bring to a boil, then reduce the heat to low to maintain a gentle simmer. Cover the pan partially and cook for 45 minutes. Every 15 minutes or so, check the pan to make sure there is still enough liquid for the sauce to braise; add more broth, ¼ cup (2 fl oz/60 ml) at a time, if needed. Remove from the saucepan heat. Taste and adjust the seasoning.

Use right away, or let the sauce cool completely before storing in an airtight container in the refrigerator for up to 1 week or in the freezer for up to 2 months.

MAKES ABOUT 2½ CUPS (20 FL OZ/625 ML)

2 cups (2 oz/60 g) fresh basil leaves, packed

2 cloves garlic

¼ cup (1½ oz/45 g) pine nuts, toasted

½ cup (4 fl oz/125 ml) extra-virgin olive oil

Kosher salt and freshly ground pepper

½ cup (2 oz/60 g) freshly grated
Parmesan cheese

CLASSIC BASIL PESTO

In a food processor or blender, combine the basil, garlic, and pine nuts. Pulse until the ingredients are uniformly minced, scraping down the sides of the bowl or jar as needed.

With the machine running, slowly drizzle in the olive oil and process until smooth and well combined. Season with salt and pepper. Transfer the pesto to a bowl and stir in the cheese.

Use right away, or store in an airtight container in the refrigerator for up to 2 weeks or in the freezer for up to 2 months.

MAKES ABOUT 1 CUP (8 FL OZ/250 ML)

GARDEN-FRESH SAUCE

Homemade basil pesto is a wonderfully flavorful and aromatic sauce. This is a great recipe to get the kids involved as little hands love to pluck basil leaves from stems. Pesto freezes well, so double the recipe for another dinner. For variations, substitute lemon basil, kale, or arugula for the regular basil. For a savory snack, spread leftover pesto on a slice of grilled Italian bread and top with a fried egg and shredded mozzarella.

2 tablespoons olive oil

½ yellow onion, chopped

2 cloves garlic, minced

¼ teaspoon red pepper flakes (optional)

6 tablespoons (3 fl oz/90 ml) vodka

1 can (28 oz/875 g) crushed tomatoes

Kosher salt and freshly ground pepper

¼ cup (2 fl oz/60 ml) heavy cream

2 tablespoons chopped fresh basil

TOMATO VODKA-CREAM SAUCE

INDULGE A LITTLE

Tomatoes, vodka, and cream simmered together create a rich and creamy sauce that's terrific with just about any shape of pasta. The vodka flavor is distinct but subtle, nicely mellowed after low-heat simmering.

Warm the olive oil in a heavy-bottomed, nonreactive saucepan over medium-high heat. Add the onion and sauté until translucent, about 4 minutes. Add the garlic and the red pepper flakes, if using, and sauté just until the garlic is soft, about 1 minute longer. Add the vodka and cook until the liquid is reduced by about half, about 3 minutes.

Stir in the tomatoes with their juice and season with salt and pepper. Bring to a boil, then reduce the heat to low and simmer for 20 minutes, stirring occasionally. Stir in the cream and the basil and simmer for about 5 minutes longer. Remove from the heat. Taste and adjust the seasoning.

Use right away, or let the sauce cool completely before storing in an airtight container in the refrigerator for up to 5 days or in the freezer for up to 2 months.

MAKES ABOUT 3 CUPS (24 FL OZ/750 ML)

2 cups (16 fl oz/500 ml) heavy cream

½ cup (4 oz/125 g) unsalted butter

1 cup (4 oz/125 g) freshly grated
Parmesan cheese

Kosher salt and freshly ground pepper

Freshly grated nutmeg

ALFREDO SAUCE

In a saucepan, warm the cream over medium-low heat. In another saucepan, melt
the butter over medium heat. Add the warmed heavy cream and stir in the cheese.
Season with salt, pepper, and a small pinch of nutmeg.

Bring the sauce to a gentle simmer and cook just until it thickens slightly, about
2 minutes. Alfredo will continue to cook even after you remove it from the heat,
so be careful not to overcook it or your sauce will become too thick.

Use right away, or let the sauce cool completely before storing in an airtight container
in the refrigerator for up to 2 days. Do not freeze.

MAKES ABOUT 2¼ CUPS (18 FL OZ/560 ML)

CREAMY DECADENCE

This classic cream-based sauce
tastes luxurious, but is so simple
to prepare. Alfredo is best made
the night you plan to serve it,
as it can thicken too much when
it cools. You can add more heavy
cream, one tablespoon at a time,
during cooking until you reach the
desired consistency. For a fresh
twist, swirl in the grated zest of
one lemon just before serving.

PASTA

vegetarian • meat • seafood • baked

3¾ cups (19 oz/590 g) all-purpose flour, plus more for kneading

4 large eggs

Extra-virgin olive oil

Kosher salt

BASIC PASTA DOUGH

Place the flour in a mound on a wooden countertop or a plastic surface (stainless steel or marble surfaces are cold and can reduce the elasticity of the dough). Make a well in the flour and break the eggs into it.

Add a drizzle of olive oil and a pinch of salt to the well. Beat the eggs with a fork, pushing around the edges with your other hand to make sure no egg runs out, and pulling flour from the sides of the mounds into the eggs.

When you have pulled in enough flour to form a ball too stiff to beat with the fork, start kneading the dough with the palm of your hand, incorporating as much flour as you can. (You may have up to ¾ cup/4 oz/125 g leftover flour.) You should now have a big ball of dough and a bunch of tiny, crumbly balls that have not been incorporated. Push these aside and scrape the surface with a metal spatula.

Sprinkle the clean surface with flour, place the dough on top, and knead by pushing it down and away from you, stretching it out. Fold the dough in half and continue pushing it down and away. Keep repeating this action until the dough no longer feels sticky and has a smooth surface. This should take about 15 minutes. (This process is important for a delicate, elastic pasta, so don't rush.) Add more flour if the dough continues to feel sticky. When the dough is smooth, wrap in plastic wrap and let rest for 30 minutes at room temperature to relax the dough before rolling out.

Cut the dough into 4 pieces to make it easier to roll out. See rolling instructions at right.

MAKES ABOUT 1 POUND (500 G) FRESH PASTA

Run 1 piece of dough through the widest setting on a pasta machine 2 or 3 times. Flour the dough lightly if starts to stick. Fold the dough into thirds, go to the next narrower setting, and run the dough through again, then repeat this twice. The pasta should become longer, thinner, and more even. Fold, flour, and run the dough 2 or 3 times through each progressively narrower setting until you have a long, thin, smooth sheet of pasta. Cut into the desired shape.

1½ lb (750 g) very ripe cherry or plum tomatoes, halved or quartered

3 cloves garlic, minced

½ cup (4 fl oz/125 ml) olive oil, plus more for drizzling

2 tablespoons red wine vinegar

½ teaspoon kosher salt, plus more for the water

¼ teaspoon freshly ground pepper

12 oz (375 g) spaghetti

¼ cup (⅓ oz/10 g) chopped or torn fresh basil

¼ cup (1 oz/30 g) freshly grated Parmesan cheese

12 oz (375 g) burrata cheese, at room temperature

SPAGHETTI WITH TOMATOES, BASIL & BURRATA

CAPRESE PASTA

————→>>>>>>>>>

This pasta features the same main ingredients as the iconic salad. The key to its success is using very ripe tomatoes. During winter months, sundried tomatoes can be substituted. Burrata is an Italian cheese made from mozzarella and cream that's easy to tear; if you can't find burrata, substitute fresh mozzarella.

In a large, nonreactive bowl, combine the tomatoes, garlic, olive oil, vinegar, salt, and pepper. Let stand at room temperature, stirring once in a while, for 1 hour.

Bring a large pot of generously salted water to a boil over high heat. Add the spaghetti and cook according to the package directions. Drain the pasta well and add, while still piping hot, to the bowl with the tomatoes. Stir in the basil and Parmesan. Taste and adjust the seasoning.

Divide the pasta among bowls and top each serving with 2–3 oz (60–90 g) of the burrata. Drizzle the bowls with olive oil and serve right away.

SERVES 4–6

Kosher salt and freshly ground pepper

1 lb (500 g) asparagus, trimmed and cut into 2-inch (5-cm) pieces

1 clove garlic

1 cup (1 oz/30 g) spinach leaves, tough stems removed

¼ cup (1 oz/30 g) walnuts, toasted

½ cup (2 oz/60 g) freshly grated Parmesan cheese

¼ cup (2 fl oz/60 ml) olive oil

2 teaspoons lemon juice

8 oz (250 g) rigatoni

4 oz (125 g) ricotta salata cheese, shaved with a vegetable peeler

RIGATONI WITH ASPARAGUS PESTO & RICOTTA SALATA

Bring a large pot of generously salted water to a boil over high heat. Add the asparagus and cook just until fork-tender, 2–3 minutes. Using a slotted spoon, transfer the asparagus to a colander and rinse under cold water. Reserve the pot with the water.

Set about one-fourth of the asparagus aside and add the remainder to a food processor. Add the garlic, spinach, walnuts, and Parmesan and process until finely chopped. With the machine running, drizzle in the olive oil and process until well combined. Stir in the lemon juice and season with salt and pepper.

Bring the large pot of water you used to cook the asparagus back to a boil over high heat. Add the rigatoni and cook according to the package directions. Drain well and transfer to a large bowl. Stir in the asparagus pesto and the reserved asparagus pieces. Taste and adjust the seasoning. Transfer to a serving bowl and garnish with the ricotta salata shavings. Serve right away.

SERVES 4

SPRINGTIME PESTO

This innovative variation of classic pesto calls for fresh asparagus and walnuts. The addition of spinach gives the pesto its bright green color. Like other pesto-based pasta dishes, this one tastes great served warm or cold making it a good choice for a picnic or buffet. For a hit of color, add some yellow and red cherry tomatoes just before serving.

1 small Italian eggplant, cut into ½-inch (12-mm) pieces

¼ cup (2 fl oz/60 ml) olive oil, plus 1 teaspoon

Kosher salt and freshly ground black pepper

¼ teaspoon red pepper flakes

1¼ cups (10 fl oz/310 ml) Marinara Sauce (page 16)

12 oz (375 g) rigatoni

8 oz (250 g) fresh mozzarella chese, preferably buffalo, cut into ½-inch (12-mm) cubes

6 fresh basil leaves

RIGATONI WITH ROASTED EGGPLANT & SPICY MARINARA

This rustic Italian classic is full of flavor and comes together quickly for a weeknight meal. You can omit the crushed red pepper flakes, or serve them on the side, if you have guests or family members that don't like spicy foods. Serve this dish with a glass of chianti and a Chicory Salad with Roasted Pears, Stilton & Almonds (page 110) for a great pairing.

Preheat the oven to 400°F (200°C).

Pile the eggplant on a baking sheet lined with parchment paper. Drizzle with the ¼ cup (2 fl oz/60 ml) olive oil, season well with salt and black pepper, and toss to coat. Spread the eggplant in a single layer and roast, stirring once about halfway through, until fork-tender, 20–25 minutes. Remove from the oven and set aside.

Warm the 1 teaspoon olive oil in a saucepan. Add the red pepper flakes and sauté just until toasted, about 30 seconds. Add the marinara sauce and stir until warmed through.

Meanwhile, bring a large pot of generously salted water to a boil over high heat. Add the rigatoni and cook according to the package directions. Drain well and transfer to a large bowl. Stir in the marinara, eggplant, and mozzarella. Tear the basil leaves and stir into the pasta. Taste and adjust the seasoning. Serve right away.

SERVES 4–6

6 tablespoons (3 fl oz/90 ml) olive oil, plus more for drizzling

3 yellow onions, halved and sliced

Kosher salt and freshly ground pepper

1 teaspoon balsamic vinegar

3 cloves garlic, minced

10 oz (315 g) spinach leaves, tough stems removed

1 can (15 oz/470 g) cannellini beans, rinsed and drained

12 oz (375 g) fettuccine

6 tablespoons (1½ oz/45 g) freshly grated Parmesan cheese

FETTUCCINE WITH SPINACH, ONIONS & WHITE BEANS

Warm 2 tablespoons of the olive oil in a large frying pan over high heat. Add the onions and sauté until translucent, about 6 minutes. Reduce the heat to medium-low and season well with salt and pepper. Cook slowly, stirring often, until the onions turn golden brown, 30–35 minutes. Add the vinegar and stir until completely absorbed, about 2 minutes. Transfer the onions to a bowl and set aside; do not wipe the pan clean.

Return the same pan to the stove top over medium-high heat. Warm 1 tablespoon of the olive oil and add the garlic. Sauté just until soft, about 1 minute. Add the spinach, season with salt and pepper, and sauté until just wilted, about 3 minutes. Return the onions to the pan and add the beans. Cook, stirring, just until the beans are warmed through, about 2 minutes.

Meanwhile, bring a large pot of generously salted water to a boil over high heat. Add the fettuccine and cook according to the package directions. Drain the pasta, reserving ½ cup (4 fl oz/125 ml) of the cooking water, and add the pasta to the frying pan. Add 4 tablespoons (1 oz/30 g) of the Parmesan, the reserved pasta-cooking water, and the remaining 3 tablespoons olive oil. Cook just until the sauce thickens a bit, about 2 minutes. Season with salt and pepper and transfer to a shallow serving bowl. Top with the remaining 2 tablespoons Parmesan, drizzle with olive oil, and serve right away.

SERVES 4–6

Pairing pasta with beans is a traditional combination in Italy and an easy way to add meatless protein to a meal. Caramelize an extra onion when making this dish then use it to top roasted chicken or add to a frittata for another supper during the week.

1 zucchini, halved lengthwise and cut crosswise into half-moons

1 red bell pepper, seeded and cut into ½-inch (12-mm) pieces

1 yellow bell pepper, seeded and cut into ½-inch (12-mm) pieces

2 tablespoons olive oil

Kosher salt and freshly ground pepper

2 carrots, peeled, cut into thin slices on the bias

1 tablespoon unsalted butter

1 cup (4 oz/125 g) plain dried bread crumbs

12 oz (375 g) gemelli

1½ cups (12 fl oz/375 ml) Alfredo Sauce (page 25), warmed

1 cup (6 oz/185 g) cherry tomatoes, halved

PASTA PRIMAVERA WITH BUTTERY BREAD CRUMBS

Preheat the oven to 400°F (200°C).

Pile the zucchini and bell peppers on a baking sheet. Drizzle with 1 tablespoon of the olive oil, season with salt and pepper, and toss to coat. Spread the vegetables in a single layer and roast, stirring once about halfway through, until soft, about 8 minutes. Transfer to a large bowl. On the same baking sheet, toss the carrots with the remaining 1 tablespoon olive oil, season with salt and pepper, and spread in a single layer. Roast, stirring once, until fork-tender, about 12 minutes. Transfer to the bowl with the other vegetables. Set aside.

Bring a large pot of generously salted water to a boil over high heat.

Meanwhile, melt the butter in a frying pan over medium-high heat. Add the bread crumbs and stir to coat. Season with salt and pepper and sauté until lightly toasted, about 2 minutes. Remove from the heat and set aside.

Add the gemelli to the boiling water and cook according to the package directions. Drain well and add to the bowl with the vegetables. Stir in the alfredo sauce and the cherry tomatoes. Taste and adjust the seasoning. Transfer to a serving dish, top with the buttery bread crumbs, and serve right away.

SERVES 4–6

VEGETARIAN DELIGHT

━◄◄◄◄◄◄◄◄◄━

This kid-friendly recipe is packed with colorful vegetables but you can use any combination you want. Buttery bread crumbs add crunch and texture to this creamy dish. For a lighter variation, skip the sauce and substitute with extra-virgin olive oil, freshly grated Parmesan cheese, and fresh basil.

Kosher salt and freshly ground pepper

2 tablespoons olive oil, plus more for drizzling

3 cloves garlic, minced

1½ lb (750 g) white or brown mushrooms, brushed clean and quartered

1 tablespoon finely chopped fresh rosemary

¾ cup (12 fl oz/375 ml) low-sodium vegetable broth

12 oz (375 g) tagliatelle

6 tablespoons (3 oz/90 g) mascarpone cheese, at room temperature

2 tablespoons freshly grated Parmesan cheese

Zest of 1 lemon

TAGLIATELLE WITH MUSHROOMS, ROSEMARY & MASCARPONE

SILKY & LEMONY

Mascarpone contributes a luxurious taste and silky texture to this otherwise simple pasta. Adding the cheese at room temperature helps it to combine more easily. To clean the mushrooms, simply wipe them with a paper towel (running them under water can cause sogginess).

Bring a large pot of generously salted water to a boil.

Meanwhile, warm the 2 tablespoons olive oil in a large frying pan over medium-high heat. Add the garlic and sauté just until soft, about 1 minute. Add the mushrooms and rosemary and season well with salt and pepper. Sauté until the mushrooms are soft and browned around the edges, about 6 minutes. Add the broth, season again with salt and pepper, raise the heat to high, and cook until the liquid is reduced by about half, about 4 minutes. Keep warm over very low heat.

Add the tagliatelle to the boiling water and cook according to the package instructions. Drain well and transfer to a large bowl. Carefully pour the mushrooms with all of the broth over the top of the pasta. Stir in the mascarpone, Parmesan, and lemon zest. Taste and adjust the seasoning and transfer to a serving platter. Finish with a final drizzle of olive oil and serve right away.

SERVES 4–6

Kosher salt and freshly ground pepper

1 small head cauliflower, about 1¼ lb (625 g)

6 tablespoons (3 fl oz/90 ml) olive oil

½ yellow onion, chopped

2 cloves garlic, chopped

¾ cup (6 fl oz/180 ml) low-sodium vegetable or chicken broth

12 oz (375 g) penne

¼ cup (⅓ oz/10 g) chopped fresh basil

3 tablespoons freshly grated Parmesan cheese

½ cup (2 oz/60 g) plain dried bread crumbs

PENNE WITH CAULIFLOWER-GARLIC SAUCE

Bring a large pot of salted water to a boil over high heat. Core the cauliflower and chop into small florets. You should have about 4 cups (8 oz/250 g). Carefully drop the florets into the boiling water and cook for 5 minutes. Drain well and set aside.

Refill the pot with water, salt generously, and bring to a boil over high heat.

Meanwhile, warm 4 tablespoons (2 fl oz/60 ml) of the olive oil in a large frying pan over medium-high heat. Add the onion and sauté until translucent, about 5 minutes. Add the garlic and the cauliflower and season well with salt and pepper. Sauté until the cauliflower is quite soft, about 8 minutes. Add the broth and bring to a gentle simmer. Season again with salt and pepper, cover, and cook for about 10 minutes to allow the flavors to blend. Keep warm over very low heat while you cook the pasta.

Add the penne to the boiling water and cook according to the package directions. Reserve ½ cup (4 fl oz/125 ml) of the cooking water and drain well. Transfer the pasta to a large serving bowl and stir in the cauliflower mixture, the reserved cooking water, the basil, and the cheese. Taste and adjust the seasoning. Drizzle on the remaining 2 tablespoons olive oil, sprinkle evenly with the bread crumbs, and serve right away.

SERVES 4–6

HEALTHY CHOICE

Here, chopped cauliflower is cooked with olive oil and garlic to produce a light and delicious sauce. Because the sauce is fairly thick, top the pasta quickly before the sauce has a chance to cool. If it gets too thick, just add at little more pasta water to thin out the consistency. For variations, add chopped cherry tomatoes, asparagus tips, or a couple of handfuls of spinach to the sauce during the last 5 minutes of cooking.

Kosher salt and freshly ground pepper

12 oz (375 g) pennette

6 tablespoons (3 fl oz/90 ml) olive oil

1 red onion, halved and sliced

3 cloves garlic, minced

2 bunches kale, tough stems and center spines removed, chopped

1 cup (8 fl oz/250 ml) low-sodium vegetable or chicken broth

5 oz (155 g) feta cheese, crumbled (about 1 cup)

Zest of 1 lemon

PENNETTE WITH KALE & FETA

Feta adds a wonderful salty flavor to this unexpected and delicious dish. You can substitute any leafy green for the kale, such as swiss chard, spinach, or arugula. To add some crunch, top this dish with a handful of toasted pine nuts. Serve with Garlicky Roasted Mushrooms (page 116).

Bring a large pot of generously salted water to a boil. Cook the pennette according to the package instructions. Reserve ½ cup (4 fl oz/125 ml) of the cooking water and drain well. Set aside.

In a large frying over medium-high heat, warm 2 tablespoons of the olive oil. Add the onion, season with salt and pepper, and cook, stirring often, until golden brown, about 8 minutes. Add the garlic and cook just until soft, about 1 minute longer. Add the kale, season with salt and pepper, and sauté until the leaves begin to wilt, about 2 minutes. Add the broth and cook until about half of the liquid is absorbed, about 3 minutes.

Add the pasta and the reserved cooking water to the pan and stir until warmed through. Stir in the remaining 4 tablespoons (2 fl oz/60 ml) olive oil. Taste and adjust the seasoning, keeping in mind that your feta may be quite salty. Transfer the pasta to a serving bowl and stir in the feta and lemon zest. Serve right away.

SERVES 4–6

¾ lb (375 g) Yukon gold potatoes, peeled and cut into very small dice

Kosher salt and freshly ground pepper

4 oz (125 g) slender green beans or haricots verts, trimmed

12 oz (375 g) cavatappi or small tubular pasta

1 recipe Pesto (page 21)

2 tablespoons freshly grated Parmesan cheese

Olive oil for drizzling

CAVATAPPI WITH PESTO, POTATOES & GREEN BEANS

Put the potatoes in a large saucepan and add cold water to cover by 2 inches (5 cm). Place over high heat, add 2 teaspoons salt, and bring to a boil. Reduce the heat to medium-low and cook until the potatoes are fork-tender, about 12 minutes. Using a slotted spoon, transfer the potatoes to a large bowl.

Let the water return to a boil. Add the green beans and cook until just tender, about 2 minutes. Drain and add to the bowl with the potatoes.

Bring a large pot of generously salted water to a boil over high heat. Add the cavatappi and cook according to the package directions. Drain well and add to the bowl with the vegetables. Add the pesto and stir to combine. Stir in the Parmesan and season with salt and pepper. Transfer to a serving bowl, drizzle with olive oil, and serve right away.

SERVES 4-6

VERSATILE CHOICE

This striking dish is equally tasty warm or cold, making it a great choice for an indoor or outdoor meal. Be sure to add the sauce to the potatoes and pasta while they are still warm so that they will absorb more sauce and flavor. If you want a protein to go with this meal, try grilled Italian sausage.

2 tablespoons olive oil, plus more for greasing

1 shallot, minced

2 cloves garlic, minced

Kosher salt and freshly ground pepper

1 large butternut squash, about 1½ lb (750 g), peeled, seeded, and cut into ½-inch (12-mm) dice (about 3 cups/115 oz/460 g), boiled for 10 minutes

Freshly grated nutmeg

1 large egg, separated

48 square wonton wrappers

¾ cup (6 oz/185 g) unsalted butter

12–15 fresh sage leaves

½ cup (2 oz/60 g) freshly grated Parmesan cheese

BUTTERNUT SQUASH RAVIOLI WITH SAGE & BROWNED BUTTER

Incredibly delicious and perhaps the fastest sauce you'll ever make, sage-infused brown butter is a great accompaniment to this ravioli. Butternut squash can be replaced with sweet potatoes or carrots. The uncooked ravioli can be frozen; when ready to consume, place the frozen ravioli into boiling water, as directed, and increase the boiling time by about 2 minutes, or until the wonton wrappers are soft.

Warm the olive oil in a frying pan over medium-high heat. Add the shallot and cook until translucent, about 3 minutes. Add the garlic and cook just until soft, about 1 minute longer. Add the squash and stir to coat with the oil. Remove from the heat and, using a potato masher or a large fork, mash the squash until smooth. Season with nutmeg, salt, and pepper. Transfer to a small bowl and stir in the egg yolk. Set aside.

Bring a large pot of generously salted water to a boil over high heat. Put the egg white in a small bowl and beat it with a fork. On a clean work surface, lay down 24 of the wonton wrappers. Using a pastry brush, brush the edges of each wrapper with the beaten egg white. Place a heaping teaspoon of the squash filling in the middle of each wrapper. Top each with another wrapper, pressing firmly to seal the edges and taking care to press out any air bubbles.

Turn down the heat under the boiling water to medium. (You don't want to cook ravioli in rapidly boiling water because they are likely to explode.) Gently lower the ravioli into the boiling water, 6 at a time, and cook until the wonton wrappers are soft, about 4 minutes per batch. Using a slotted spoon, transfer each batch of ravioli to an oiled baking sheet.

Melt the butter in a large frying pan over medium-high heat. Once the butter has melted, add the sage leaves. Cook until the sage leaves are crisp and the butter is brown, about 3 minutes. Carefully add the ravioli to the pan, 6 at a time, and turn very gently to coat with the brown butter. Transfer the ravioli to a serving dish. Top with the remaining butter and sage leaves in the pan, sprinkle with the Parmesan, and season with salt and pepper. Serve right away.

SERVES 6

6 slices thick-cut bacon, chopped

2 cloves garlic, minced

2 large eggs, at room temperature

½ cup (2 oz/60 g) freshly grated
Parmesan cheese, plus 2 tablespoons

Kosher salt and freshly ground pepper

12 oz (375 g) bucatini

2 tablespoons chopped fresh flat-leaf parsley

BUCATINI ALLA CARBONARA

Heat a frying pan over medium-high heat and add the bacon. Cook, stirring often, until crisp, about 6 minutes total. Using a slotted spoon, transfer the bacon to a large bowl. Remove the pan from the heat and add the garlic to the bacon grease in the pan. Let the garlic soften in the residual heat, about 30 seconds. Using a slotted spoon, transfer the garlic to the bowl with the bacon.

Beat the eggs in a small bowl and stir in the ½ cup (2 oz/60 g) Parmesan. Set aside.

Bring a large pot of generously salted water to a boil over high heat. Add the bucatini and cook according to the package directions. Drain the pasta, reserving ½ cup (4 fl oz/125 ml) of the cooking water. Add the pasta to the bowl with the bacon and immediately stir in the egg mixture. Add the reserved pasta-cooking water and stir to combine. Stir in the 2 tablespoons Parmesan and the parsley. Season with salt and pepper and serve right away.

SERVES 4-6

FAMILY FAVORITE

This simple recipe is always a crowd pleaser. It's also a great go-to dinner for a busy weeknight as most of the ingredients are pantry staples. Be sure to add the egg to hot pasta so that the heat will cook it. Have all your ingredients ready to go before boiling the pasta.

Kosher salt and freshly ground pepper

1 lb (500 g) asparagus, tough woody ends snapped or cut off, cut into 1-inch (2.5-cm) pieces

5 oz (155 g) pancetta, chopped

½ yellow onion, chopped

12 oz (375 g) orecchiette

6 tablespoons (3 fl oz/90 ml) olive oil

¼ cup (1 oz/30 g) freshly grated Parmesan cheese

3 oz (90 g) goat cheese, at room temperature, cut or broken into 1-inch (2.5-cm) pieces

2 tablespoons pine nuts, toasted

PANCETTA, ASPARAGUS & GOAT CHEESE ORECCHIETTE

Chopped pancetta and little pine nuts nestle perfectly into this small ear-shaped pasta. Cut vibrant asparagus on the bias for a simple way to elevate the appearance of this dish. Enveloped in the creamy mixture of goat cheese and Parmesan, this dish is as delicious as it is easy.

Bring a large pot of generously salted water to a boil over high heat. Add the asparagus and cook just until barely fork-tender, about 3 minutes. Using a slotted spoon, transfer the asparagus to a plate and set aside. Return the water to a boil.

In a frying pan over medium-high heat, cook the pancetta, stirring occasionally, until crisp and cooked through, about 5 minutes. Using a slotted spoon, transfer the pancetta to paper towels to drain. Do not wipe the pan clean. Add the onion to the fat in the pan and season with salt and pepper. Sauté until lightly browned and soft, about 5 minutes.

Add the orecchiette to the boiling water and cook according to the package instructions. Drain the pasta, reserving ½ cup (4 fl oz/125 ml) of the cooking water, and set aside.

Add the olive oil to the pan and stir in the asparagus, pancetta, and reserved pasta-cooking water. Add the orecchiette and stir to mix well. Cook until the sauce in the pan thickens just a bit, about 2 minutes. Stir in the Parmesan, goat cheese, and pine nuts. Season with salt and pepper and serve right away.

SERVES 4–6

WHAT YOU NEED

2 tablespoons olive oil, plus more for greasing

½ yellow onion, finely chopped

2 cloves garlic, minced

1 tablespoon fennel seed

½ lb (500 g) *each* ground beef and pork

1 large egg

¼ cup (½ oz/15 g) plain fresh bread crumbs

Kosher salt and freshly ground pepper

1¼ cups (10 fl oz/310 ml) Marinara Sauce (page 16)

12 oz (375 g) spaghetti

¼ cup (⅓ oz/10 g) chopped fresh basil (optional)

Freshly grated Parmesan cheese for serving

CLASSIC SPAGHETTI & MEATBALLS

Preheat the oven to 350°F (180°C).

Warm the olive oil in a frying pan over medium-high heat. Add the onion, garlic, and fennel seed and sauté until the onion begins to soften, 3–4 minutes. Transfer the onion mixture to a large bowl and the add the beef, pork, egg, bread crumbs, 2 teaspoons salt, and 1 teaspoon pepper. Using your hands, mix until roughly combined (do not overmix). Form the meat mixture into balls about the size of small golf balls, arranging them in a single layer on an oiled baking sheet as you work. Bake until cooked through, about 25 minutes.

While the meatballs are baking, gently warm the marinara sauce in a large saucepan over medium heat. When the meatballs are done, add them to the sauce and stir gently until all the meatballs are well coated with sauce. Reduce the heat to very low and cover to keep warm.

Bring a large pot of generously salted water to a boil over high heat. Add the spaghetti and cook according to the package directions. Drain well and transfer to a large serving bowl. Carefully pour the meatballs with the sauce over the pasta and garnish with the basil, if using. Serve right away, passing the Parmesan at the table.

SERVES 4–6

CLASSIC SUPPER

A bowl of marinara-tossed spaghetti topped with plump meatballs is a family dinner favorite. These meatballs call for a combination of beef and pork for extra flavor but you can also make them with ground chicken, turkey, or veal. Make a double batch of meatballs and freeze half of them for another meal. For a variation, serve the meatballs with Amatriciana Sauce (page 17) on a bed of couscous, which is actually tiny pearls of pasta.

1 lb (500 g) Brussels sprouts, quartered

6 tablespoons (3 fl oz/90 ml) olive oil

2 tablespoons balsamic vinegar

Kosher salt and freshly ground pepper

6 slices thick-cut bacon

12 oz (375 g) ditalini

1 yellow onion, quartered and sliced

1 cup (8 fl oz/250 ml) low-sodium chicken broth

½ cup (2 oz/60 g) freshly grated pecorino romano cheese

Zest of 1 lemon

DITALINI WITH BRUSSELS SPROUTS, BACON & PECORINO

PASTA PERFECTION

Brussels sprouts with bacon, a popular combination, transforms this humble pasta dish into something spectacular. If you're using larger Brussels sprouts, cut them into 6 or 8 pieces. You don't want them to be too big next to the small ditalini. Finish this dish in the pan in which you fried the bacon for maximum flavor.

Preheat the oven to 400°F (200°C).

Pile the brussels sprouts on a baking sheet lined with parchment paper. Drizzle with 4 tablespoons (2 fl oz/60 ml) of the olive oil, and the vinegar, and toss to coat. Season with salt and pepper. Spread the sprouts in a single layer and roast, stirring once about halfway through, until fork-tender and caramelized, about 25 minutes. Set aside.

Bring a large pot of generously salted water to a boil over high heat.

In a large frying pan over medium-high heat, fry the bacon until crispy, about 6 minutes. Transfer to paper towels to drain. When cool enough to handle, break the bacon into bite-sized piece.

Meanwhile, add the ditalini to the boiling water and cook according to the package instructions. Drain well and set aside.

Discard all but about 1 tablespoon of the bacon grease in the pan, add the remaining 2 tablespoons olive oil, and warm over medium-high heat. Add the onion, season with salt and pepper, and sauté until lightly browned and soft, about 4 minutes. Add the brussels sprouts, the pasta, and the bacon and stir to combine. Stir in the chicken broth and cook until the sauce thickens just a bit, about 3 minutes. Stir in the cheese and the lemon zest. Taste and adjust the seasoning. Serve right away.

SERVES 4-6

2 tablespoons olive oil

1 boneless pork shoulder,
about 2½ lb (1.25 kg)

Kosher salt and freshly ground pepper

1 yellow onion, chopped

3 cloves garlic, minced

4 fresh thyme sprigs

1½ tablespoons fennel seed

1 cup (8 fl oz/250 ml) dry red wine

1 can (28 oz/875 g) diced tomatoes

1–3 cups (8–24 fl oz/250–750 ml) low-sodium
beef broth

1 lb (500 g) pappardelle

Freshly grated Parmesan cheese

SLOW-COOKED PORK & FENNEL RAGÙ

Preheat the oven to 325°F (165°C).

In a large Dutch oven or other heavy-bottomed, ovenproof pot with a tight-fitting lid, warm the olive oil over high heat. Season the pork shoulder well with salt and pepper. When the oil is good and hot, add the pork shoulder and sear, turning as needed, until browned on all sides, about 10 minutes total. Transfer to a large platter and set aside.

Add the onion to the pot and sauté until translucent, about 5 minutes. Add the garlic, thyme, and fennel seed and sauté just until the garlic is soft, about 2 minutes. Stir in the wine, scraping up any browned bits on the bottom of the pot, and cook until the liquid is reduced by half, about 3 minutes. Add the tomatoes and their juices and 1 cup (8 fl oz/250 ml) of the beef broth and bring to a boil. Return the pork shoulder to the pot; the liquid should come about one-third of the way up the sides of the pork. If it doesn't, add more beef broth as needed.

Transfer the pot to the oven and cook until the meat shreds easily with a fork, about 3 hours. Turn the pork every 45 minutes or so, adding a little more broth as needed if the pot seems dry. When the pork is done, remove from the oven and let cool slightly. Using 2 forks, shred the meat in the pot. Season with salt and pepper and stir well to combine.

When ready to serve, bring a large pot of generously salted water to boil over high heat. Add the pappardelle and cook according to the package directions. Drain well and transfer to a large serving bowl. Pour the pork ragù over the top of the pappardelle, top with the Parmesan, and serve right away.

SERVES 8–10

WEEKEND SPECIAL

This dish takes time to prepare, but it's worth the wait and your house will smell divine while it cooks. The recipe makes enough sauce to cover at least two meals. Pull together the recipe on Saturday or Sunday then enjoy the second meal later in the week. The hearty pork is also delicious served on a soft roll for an Italian-style sandwich.

2 boneless, skinless chicken breast halves, about ¾ lb (375 g) each

1 tablespoon olive oil

Kosher salt and freshly ground pepper

½ bunch broccoli rabe, thick stems removed

12 oz (375 g) fettuccine

1 cup (8 fl oz/250 ml) Alfredo Sauce (page 25), warmed

Zest of 1 lemon

2 tablespoons chopped fresh flat-leaf parsley

FETTUCCINE ALFREDO WITH CHICKEN & BROCCOLI RABE

Be careful not to overcook this creamy sauce or it could become too thick; it will continue to thicken as it cools. You can make this dish with different vegetables throughout the year; try cubed and roasted sweet potatoes, blanched asparagus, or roasted red peppers. Balance this hearty dish out with a side of Lemony Sautéed Kale with Garlic & Golden Raisins (page 118).

Preheat the oven to 375°F (190°C).

Put the chicken in a baking dish. Brush with the olive oil and season all over with salt and pepper. Bake until opaque throughout, about 25 minutes. Transfer to a cutting board and, when cool enough to handle, cut into 1-inch (2.5-cm) slices. Transfer to a large bowl and set aside.

Bring a pot of generously salted water to a boil over high heat. Add the broccoli rabe and cook until al dente, about 4 minutes. Using a slotted spoon, transfer to a clean cutting board. When cool enough to handle, cut into 1-inch (2.5-cm) pieces. Add to the bowl with the chicken.

Return the pot of water to a boil and add the fettuccine. Cook according to the package directions. Drain the pasta well and add to the bowl with the chicken and broccoli rabe. Pour the alfredo sauce over the top and toss to combine. Stir in the lemon zest and parsley. Season with salt and pepper and serve right away.

SERVES 4–6

Kosher salt and freshly ground pepper

1 large egg, separated

2 cups (16 oz/500 g) whole-milk ricotta cheese

½ cup (2 oz/60 g) shredded low-moisture mozzarella cheese

¼ cup (1 oz/30 g) freshly grated pecorino romano cheese, plus more for serving

1 tablespoon chopped fresh basil

48 square wonton wrappers

1 cup (8 fl oz/250 ml) Bolognese Sauce (page 20), warmed

THREE-CHEESE BASIL RAVIOLI WITH BOLOGNESE SAUCE

Bring a large pot of generously salted water to a boil over high heat. Put the egg white in a small bowl and beat it with a fork.

In a bowl, stir together the ricotta, mozzarella, pecorino, basil, and egg yolk. Season with salt and pepper.

On a clean work surface, lay down 24 of the wonton wrappers. Brush the edges of each wrapper with the beaten egg white. Place a heaping teaspoon of the cheese filling in the middle of each wrapper. Top each with another wonton wrapper, pressing firmly to seal the edges and taking care to press out any air bubbles so your ravioli don't come apart in the water.

Turn down the heat under the boiling water to medium. (You don't want to cook ravioli in rapidly boiling water because they are likely to explode.) Gently lower the ravioli into the boiling water, 6 at a time, and cook until the wrappers are soft, about 4 minutes per batch. Using a slotted spoon, transfer each batch of ravioli to a serving platter.

When all of the ravioli are cooked, top with the bolognese sauce. Serve right away, passing more grated pecorino at the table.

SERVES 4

A simple cheese ravioli with meat sauce is always a kid-pleaser. The bolognese sauce makes this a rustic and hearty dinner, but you could use any sauce from this book for a delicious meal. Serve with Garlic Bread (page 111).

1 lb (500 g) ground turkey

¼ lb (125 g) prosciutto, finely chopped

2 cloves garlic, minced

¼ cup (½ oz/15 g) plain fresh bread crumbs

3 tablespoons chopped fresh flat-leaf parsley

1 large egg, lightly beaten

¾ cup (3 oz/90 g) freshly grated Parmesan cheese

Kosher salt and freshly ground pepper

1½ cups (12 fl oz/375 ml) Marinara Sauce (page 16)

12 oz (375 g) pennette

6 oz (185 g) bocconcini, cut into small pieces (optional)

2 tablespoons chopped fresh basil

PENNETTE WITH MINI TURKEY-PROSCIUTTO MEATBALLS

MINI MEAL

>>>>>>>>>

This "mini" take on spaghetti and meatballs is perfect for kids. Extra meatballs make tasty appetizers (or an after-school snack); serve with toothpicks alongside warm marinara.

To make the meatballs: Preheat the oven to 375°F (190°C). In a bowl, combine the turkey, prosciutto, garlic, bread crumbs, parsley, and egg. Using your hands, mix until roughly combined (do not overmix). Stir in the Parmesan, ½ teaspoon salt, and ¼ teaspoon pepper. Using your hands again, form the turkey mixture into meatballs of about 1 teaspoon each, arranging them in a single layer on an oiled baking sheet as you work. Repeat until all the meatballs are formed. Bake until cooked through, 12–15 minutes.

While the meatballs are baking, bring a large pot of generously salted water to a boil over high heat.

Gently warm the marinara sauce in a large saucepan over medium heat. When the meatballs are done, add them to the sauce and stir gently until all the meatballs are well coated with sauce. Reduce the heat to very low and cover to keep warm.

Add the pasta to the boiling water and cook according to the package directions. Drain well and transfer to a large serving bowl. Add the warm sauce and meatballs and toss to mix well. Stir in the bocconcini and basil, season with salt and pepper, and serve right away.

SERVES 4–6

Kosher salt

1 lb (500 g) sweet Italian sausage,
casings removed

12 oz (375 g) fusilli

3 tablespoons olive oil,
plus more for drizzling

1 red bell pepper, seeded and
cut into 1-inch (2.5-cm) pieces

1 yellow bell pepper, seeded and
cut into 1-inch (2.5-cm) pieces

4 cloves garlic, minced

1 cup (8 fl oz/250 ml) low-sodium
chicken broth

¼ cup (1 oz/30 g) freshly grated
Parmesan cheese

¼ cup (⅓ oz/10 g) torn fresh basil

SAUSAGE & PEPPERS WITH FUSILLI

Bring a large pot of generously salted water to a boil over high heat.

Warm a large frying pan over medium-high heat. Add the sausage and cook, stirring occasionally and using your spoon to break up any clumps, until cooked through, about 8 minutes. Using a slotted spoon, transfer the sausage to paper towels to drain.

Meanwhile, add the fusilli to the boiling water and cook according to the package directions. Drain well and set aside.

Pour off the grease from the pan and discard, but do not wipe the pan clean. Return the pan to the stove top and warm the 3 tablespoons olive oil over medium-high heat. Add the bell peppers and sauté until they begin to soften, about 3 minutes. Add the garlic and continue to cook, stirring often, just until the peppers are fork-tender, about 5 minutes longer.

Add the pasta, the sausage, and the broth to the pan and stir to mix well. Cook until the broth is boiling. Stir in the Parmesan and basil. Give the pasta one last drizzle of olive oil and serve right away.

SERVES 4 6

Yellow and red bell peppers are packed with vitamins and make for a colorful presentation in this simple, delicious, and healthy dish. The recipe calls for sweet Italian sausage but you can also use spicy Italian, kielbasa, chorizo or chicken apple sausage to mix things up. Make some extra sausage and peppers to wrap in a tortilla for a great lunch box treat the next day.

2 tablespoons olive oil

1 yellow onion, chopped

1 carrot, peeled and cut
into ¼-inch (6-mm) dice

1 rib celery, cut into ¼-inch (6-mm) dice

Kosher salt and freshly ground pepper

2 cloves garlic, minced

2 fresh thyme sprigs

5 cups (40 fl oz/1.25 l) low-sodium beef broth

9 oz (280 g) cheese tortellini

Freshly grated pecorino romano cheese
for garnish

TORTELLINI IN BROTH

Infusing basic boxed broth
with aromatics such as garlic
and fresh thyme converts this
dish into a flavorful and elegant
soup in a matter of minutes.
Also contributing to the quick
cook time of this dish, are
purchased tortellini, which can
be found in the refrigerated
section or pasta aisle of grocery
stores. The ease of this dish
makes it a perfect solution
for last-minute entertaining.

Warm the olive oil in a large, heavy-bottomed saucepan over medium heat. Add the onion, carrot, and celery and season well with salt and pepper. Sauté until the vegetables are soft, 6–8 minutes.

Add the garlic and thyme sprigs and sauté just until the garlic is soft, about 2 minutes. Pour in the broth, raise the heat to medium-high, and bring to a boil. Add the tortellini and cook until the pasta is al dente, about 7 minutes or according to the package directions. Discard the thyme sprigs.

Ladle the tortellini in broth into shallow bowls and garnish with the pecorino. Serve hot.

SERVES 4–6

Kosher salt and freshly ground pepper

12 oz (375 g) fettuccine

1½ cups (12 fl oz/375 ml) Alfredo Sauce
(page 25)

⅓ cup (2 oz/60 g) frozen or fresh shelled peas

Zest of 1 lemon

1 tablespoon olive oil

1 lb (500 g) sea scallops

SEARED SCALLOPS WITH CREAMY FETTUCCINE & PEAS

Bring a large pot of generously salted water to a boil over high heat. Add the fettuccine and cook according to the package directions. Ladle 1 cup (8 fl oz/250 ml) of the cooking water into a heatproof bowl and set aside. Drain the pasta in a colander, rinse under cold water, drain again, and set aside.

Rinse out the pot you cooked the pasta in and place over medium heat. Add the alfredo sauce and rewarm gently. Add the fettuccine and the peas to the sauce and toss and cook until the pasta is warmed through. If your sauce seems too thick, add the reserved pasta-cooking water, 1 tablespoon at a time, until you reach the desired consistency. Stir in the lemon zest and season with salt and pepper. Keep warm over very low heat.

Warm the olive oil in frying pan over high heat. Meanwhile, remove the tough tab of muscle (called the adductor) from the edge of each scallop, if necessary, and season them all over with salt and pepper. When the pan is very hot, add the scallops and sear just until rare, 2–3 minutes per side.

Divide the fettuccine among plates and top each with the scallops. Serve right away.

SERVES 4–6

Simple, yet elegant enough for a dinner party, this beautiful dish is a show-stopper. The trick to scallops is to make sure the pan is very hot before you add them to the pan. You want the scallops to cook fast so that they caramelize on the outside while staying moist in the middle. Wrapped up in a forkful of fettuccine and peas, lightly doused in a creamy, lemony sauce, these scallops complete a delicious meal.

1 fennel bulb

3 tablespoons unsalted butter

1 carrot, peeled and minced

1 large shallot, minced

1 clove garlic, bruised

1 tablespoon minced fresh flat-leaf parsley

½ cup (4 fl oz/125 ml) dry sherry

1 cup (8 fl oz/250 ml) heavy cream

¾ lb (375 g) lump crabmeat, picked over for shell fragments and cartilage and flaked

Kosher salt and freshly ground white pepper

1 lb (500 g) fettuccine

FETTUCCINE WITH CRAB & FENNEL

The anise notes of fennel are a good match for the rich, sweet flavor of crab in this dish. Seek out the freshest premium lump crabmeat you can find; it should be moist, not dry. Since lump crabmeat comes precooked, you only need to heat it through gently in the sauce.

Cut off the stems and feathery tops and remove any bruised outer stalks from the fennel bulb. Slice off the tough bottom of the bulb, then quarter the bulb lengthwise. Cut out and discard the tough core. Remove the outer stalks and reserve for another use. Mince the light green heart of the bulb (you should have about 3 tablespoons) and set aside.

In a large pot, bring 5 qt (5 l) water to a rapid boil. While the water is heating, make the sauce. In a frying pan large enough to accommodate the pasta later, melt the butter over medium heat. Add the carrot, shallot, garlic, parsley, and minced fennel and cook gently, stirring occasionally to prevent browning, until the vegetables are thoroughly softened and aromatic, about 7 minutes. Stir in the sherry and cook gently, stirring occasionally, until most of the alcohol has evaporated, about 3 minutes. Reduce the heat to low, add the cream, and warm just until heated through, 2–3 minutes. Add the crab and stir just until heated through, about 1 minute. Remove from the heat, season with salt and white pepper, and cover to keep warm.

Just before the sauce is ready, add 2 tablespoons salt and the fettuccine to the boiling water, and cook according to the package directions. Drain well, then add the fettuccine to the sauce in the pan and toss until the strands are well coated with the sauce. Transfer to a warmed large, shallow serving bowl or individual shallow bowls. Serve right away.

SERVES 4

Kosher salt and freshly ground pepper

2 lb (1 kg) fresh fava beans in their shells

12 oz (375 g) campanelle

3 tablespoons olive oil, plus more for drizzling

2 fennel bulbs, fronds removed, cored, halved, and sliced

¾ lb (375 g) medium shrimp, peeled and deveined

2 cloves garlic, minced

1 cup (8 fl oz/250 ml) low-sodium chicken broth

¾ cup (3 oz/90 g) freshly grated Parmesan, plus more for sprinkling

2 tablespoons chopped fresh basil

CAMPANELLE WITH FENNEL, SHRIMP & FAVA BEANS

Bring a pot of lightly salted water to a boil. Shell the fava beans and add them to the boiling water. Boil until tender, about 5 minutes. Drain, rinse under cold water, and drain again. Pinch each bean to slip it from the tough inner skin. Set the beans aside.

Bring a large pot of generously salted water to a boil over high heat. Add the campanelle and cook according to the package instructions. Drain well and set aside.

Warm the 3 tablespoons olive oil in a large frying pan over medium-high heat. Add the fennel and season with salt and pepper. Sauté just until soft, about 5 minutes. Add the shrimp and cook, flipping once, until the shrimp are bright pink, about 5 minutes total. Add the garlic and sauté just until soft, about 1 minute longer.

Add the campanelle, chicken broth, the ¾ cup (3 oz/90 g) Parmesan, and fava beans and stir to mix well. Cook until the sauce thickens a bit, about 3 minutes. Stir in the basil and top with more Parmesan cheese and a final drizzle of olive oil. Serve right away.

SERVES 4-6

SPRING FEAST

Nothing announces spring like the arrival of fava beans. As a general guideline, plan on 2 lb (1 kg) of unshelled beans, which will yield about 1 cup of shelled beans. If you are short on time, or fava beans are not available, you can substitute frozen lima beans, soy beans, or edamame.

Kosher salt and freshly ground pepper

1 bunch broccolini, about ½ lb (250 g), tough ends removed

12 oz (375 g) orzo

1½ cups (12 fl oz/375 ml) low-sodium chicken broth

2 tablespoons unsalted butter

1 tablespoon olive oil

2 cloves garlic, minced

1 lb (500 g) medium shrimp, peeled and deveined

½ cup (2 oz/60 g) freshly grated Parmesan cheese

2 tablespoons chopped fresh flat-leaf parsley

ORZO WITH SHRIMP & BROCCOLINI

As a one pot dish, this can't get much easier for a weeknight dinner. You can try variations for the shrimp, such as shredded rotisserie chicken or sausage, or used blanched asparagus or peas instead of broccolini. Serve with a side of Roasted Red Pepper, Tomato & Sourdough Crouton Salad (page 121).

Bring a large pot of generously salted water to a boil over high heat. Add the broccolini and cook until fork-tender, about 3 minutes. Using a slotted spoon, transfer the broccolini to a plate, reserving the cooking water. When cool enough to handle, chop into 1-inch (2.5-cm) pieces. Set aside.

Return the pot of water to high heat and bring to a boil. Add the orzo and cook until al dente, about 2 minutes less than the package directions for doneness. Drain well and set aside.

In a small pan over low heat, warm the broth. Keep warm while you cook the shrimp.

In a large frying pan over medium-high heat, melt the butter in the olive oil. Add the garlic and sauté just until soft, about 1 minute. Add the shrimp and season well with salt and pepper. Cook, flipping once, until the shrimp are bright pink, about 5 minutes total. Using a slotted spoon, transfer the shrimp to a clean plate and set aside.

Reduce the heat to medium-low and stir in the orzo and ½ cup (4 fl oz/125 ml) of the warm broth, scraping up any browned bits on the bottom of the pan. Cook gently, stirring often, until the broth is absorbed, about 2 minutes. Repeat to add the remaining broth ½ cup at a time, allowing the liquid to be absorbed before adding more. Stir in the cheese, parsley, shrimp, and broccolini. Season with salt and pepper and serve right away.

SERVES 4-6

Kosher salt and freshly ground pepper

1 lb (500 g) linguine

4 tablespoons (2 fl oz/60 ml) olive oil, plus more for drizzling

6 cloves garlic, minced

½ cup (4 fl oz/125 ml) dry white wine

1 bottle (8 fl oz/250 ml) clam juice

5 dozen littleneck clams, scrubbed and rinsed

2 tablespoons unsalted butter

2 tablespoons chopped fresh flat-leaf parsley

1 tablespoon chopped fresh oregano

1 cup (4 oz/125 g) plus 2 tablespoons freshly grated Parmesan cheese

LINGUINE WITH CLAMS

Bring a large pot of generously salted water to a boil over high heat. Add the linguine and cook according to the package directions. Drain well and set aside.

In a large frying pan with a tight-fitting lid, warm 2 tablespoons of the olive oil over medium-high heat. Add about half of the minced garlic and sauté just until soft, about 1 minute.

Pour in the wine and clam juice and bring to a gentle simmer. Add the clams, discarding any that do not close to the touch. Cover the pan and cook, shaking the covered pan a few times, until the clams open, 6–8 minutes. Remove from the heat. Discard any clams that didn't open. Using a slotted spoon, transfer the clams to a plate or cutting board. Put 1½ dozen of the clams in their shells in a metal bowl and cover with a clean kitchen towel to keep warm. When the rest of the clams are cool enough to handle, remove the clam meat from the shells and set aside.

Strain the cooking liquid through a fine-mesh strainer into a bowl and set aside. Rinse out the pan and place it back on the stove over medium-high heat. Warm the butter and the remaining 2 tablespoons olive oil and add the remaining garlic. Cook until the garlic is just softened, about 1 minute. Add the strained broth and bring to a low simmer.

Return the cooked clam meat to the pan. Return to a low simmer and toss in the cooked pasta, the parsley, and the oregano. Cook, stirring well to incorporate, just until everything is warmed through, about 3 minutes. Transfer the pasta to a serving dish, stir in the Parmesan cheese, season with salt and pepper, and nestle all the clams in their shells into the pasta. Finish with a drizzle of olive oil and serve right away.

SERVES 6

This quick and comforting dish, redolent of garlic, herbs, and wine, will surprise you at how easily it comes together. When buying clams, they should smell like the ocean, be tightly closed, and not be chipped or cracked. It is also important to discard any clams that do not close to the touch when raw, or that do not open after cooking.

Kosher salt and freshly ground black pepper

12 oz (375 g) tagliatelle

2 teaspoons olive oil, plus 2 tablespoons

1 yellow onion, chopped

3 cloves garlic, minced

½ teaspoon dried oregano

¾–1 teaspoon red pepper flakes

½ cup (4 fl oz/125 ml) dry white wine

1 can (28 oz/875 g) plum tomatoes

1½ tablespoons tomato paste

1½ dozen medium shrimp, shelled and deveined

1½ dozen mussels, scrubbed

2 tablespoons chopped fresh flat-leaf parsley

SEAFOOD FRA DIAVOLO WITH TAGLIATELLE

SPICE IT UP

Meaning "brother devil" in Italian, fra diavolo refers to a spicy red sauce flavored with crushed red pepper flakes. Serve this dish with a cooling salad like Chicory Salad with Roasted Pears, Stilton & Almonds (page 110). For a vegetarian dish, substitute roasted vegetables—try eggplant, red peppers, and yukon gold potatoes—for the seafood.

Bring a large pot of generously salted water to a boil over high heat. Add the tagliatelle and cook according to the package directions. Drain well and toss with the 2 teaspoons olive oil to keep it from sticking. Set aside.

Warm the 2 tablespoons olive oil in a large, heavy-bottomed saucepan over medium-high heat. Add the onion and cook until translucent, about 5 minutes. Stir in the garlic and oregano. Add the red pepper flakes to taste and season with salt and black pepper. Sauté just until the garlic is soft, about 2 minutes. Add the wine and cook, stirring, until the liquid is reduced by half, about 3 minutes. Using a wooden spoon, stir in the tomatoes and tomato paste, breaking up the tomatoes with the edge of the spoon as you stir. Bring to a boil.

Add the shrimp and the mussels, discarding any mussels that do not close to the touch. Cover the pan tightly with a lid and cook, shaking the covered pan a few times, until the mussels open, about 8 minutes. Remove from the heat. Discard any mussels that didn't open. Stir in the parsley. Taste and adjust the seasoning with salt and pepper.

Transfer the pasta to a shallow serving dish. Using a large spoon, ladle the fra diavolo with the mussels and shrimp all over the top of the pasta. Serve right away.

SERVES 4-6

Kosher salt and freshly ground pepper

8 oz (250 g) angel hair pasta, broken in half

½ cup (4 fl oz/125 ml) olive oil, plus
more for drizzling

4 cloves garlic, sliced

1½ cups (9 oz/280 g) cherry tomatoes, halved

1 can (15 oz/470 g) white beans,
rinsed and drained

2 cans (6 oz/185 g each) olive oil–packed tuna

2 tablespoons freshly grated Parmesan cheese

½ cup (½ oz/15 g) lightly packed fresh
basil leaves, chopped

ANGEL HAIR WITH TUNA, WHITE BEANS, TOMATOES & BASIL

Bring a large pot of generously salted water to a boil over high heat. Add the pasta and cook according to the package instructions. Drain, reserving ½ cup (4 fl oz/125 ml) of the cooking water, and set aside.

Warm the ½ cup (4 fl oz/125 ml) olive oil in a large frying pan over medium heat. Add the garlic and sauté just until soft, about 1 minute. Add the cherry tomatoes and season with salt and pepper. Cook, stirring occasionally, just until the tomatoes begin to release their juices but aren't falling apart, about 3 minutes.

Stir in the beans and cook just until warmed throughout, about 1 minute. Add the pasta, the tuna with the oil, and the reserved pasta-cooking water and cook until the sauce thickens just a bit, about 2 minutes. Break the tuna into bite-sized pizzas with 2 forks, if necessary. Stir in the Parmesan, basil, and season with salt and pepper. Transfer the pasta to a big serving bowl and finish with a big drizzle of olive oil over the top. Serve right away.

SERVES 4–6

REVAMPED CLASSIC

Here's a modern riff on tuna noodle casserole. Use the best-quality tuna in oil for this recipe for the best results—tuna in water, while perfect for a tuna sandwich, will be too dry in this pasta. Serve this dish as soon as it is made so the ingredients stay tender and moist. A Tricolore Salad (page 119) makes a great accompaniment.

WHAT YOU NEED

Kosher salt and freshly ground pepper

2 tablespoons unsalted butter

¼ cup (2 fl oz/60 ml) olive oil, plus more for drizzling

6 large cloves garlic, minced

1 lb (500 g) medium shrimp, peeled and deveined

12 oz (375 g) linguine

¼ cup (⅓ oz/10 g) chopped fresh flat-leaf parsley

3 tablespoons freshly grated Parmesan cheese

SHRIMP SCAMPI WITH LINGUINE

Fresh shrimp is best, but you can also find good-quality shrimp frozen in 2-pound (1-kg) bags, which is great to have on hand and thaws in no time; use just the amount you need from the bag and keep the rest in the freezer.

Bring a large pot of generously salted water to a boil over high heat.

In a large frying pan over medium heat, warm the butter and the ¼ cup (2 fl oz/60 ml) olive oil. Add the garlic and sauté just until it begins to soften but not brown, about 1 minute, taking care not to let it burn.

Add the shrimp, season with salt and pepper, and raise the heat to medium-high. Cook the shrimp, flipping once about halfway through, until opaque throughout, about 5 minutes total.

Meanwhile, add the linguine to the boiling water and cook according to the package instructions. Drain, reserving ¼ cup (2 fl oz/60 ml) of the cooking water, and set aside.

Add the linguine to the frying pan and stir in the parsley and 2 tablespoons of the Parmesan. If the pasta seems dry, add the reserved pasta-cooking water, a tablespoon at a time, and let cook for another minute or two while the sauce thickens a bit.

Transfer to a serving bowl and top with a final drizzle of olive oil and the remaining 1 tablespoon Parmesan. Serve right away.

SERVES 4-6

WHAT YOU NEED

¼ cup (2 fl oz/60 ml) extra-virgin olive oil

2 shallots, finely chopped

3 large cloves garlic, finely chopped

1 teaspoon minced fresh rosemary,
or ½ teaspoon crumbled dried rosemary

¼ teaspoon red pepper flakes

¾ cup (6 oz/185 g) tomato paste

Kosher salt

½ cup (4 fl oz/125 ml) dry red wine

1 cup (8 fl oz/250 ml) bottled clam juice

1 lb (500 g) cleaned small squid,
cut into rings and tentacles

1 lb (500 g) linguine

2 tablespoons minced fresh flat-leaf parsley

LINGUINE WITH SPICY CALAMARI

In a frying pan large enough to accommodate the pasta later, warm the olive oil over medium-low heat. Add the shallots, garlic, rosemary, and red pepper and cook gently, stirring occasionally, until the shallots and garlic are softened but not colored, about 5 minutes. Add the tomato paste and stir for about 2 minutes. Add ¼ teaspoon salt and the wine and simmer until most of the wine has evaporated, about 3 minutes. Add the clam juice and continue to simmer until thickened and aromatic, about 20 minutes.

Add the squid and cook gently until tender, no more than 5 minutes. If the sauce becomes thin after cooking the squid, remove the squid with a slotted spoon to a bowl. Cook the sauce, over gentle heat, until it once again thickens, then return the squid to the pan. Taste and adjust the seasoning. Remove from the heat and cover to keep warm.

In a large pot, bring 5 qt (5 l) water to a rapid boil. Check the package directions for the cooking time, then add 2 tablespoons salt and the pasta to the boiling water, stir well, and cook, stirring occasionally, until the pasta is 1 minute shy of being al dente.

Drain the pasta, add to the sauce in the pan, and place the pan over low heat. Add the parsley and toss the pasta and sauce together for about 1 minute. Some of the sauce will be absorbed by the pasta, but plenty will remain, keeping the pasta moist. Transfer to a warmed large, shallow serving bowl or individual shallow bowls and serve right away.

SERVES 4

The secret to a good calamari dish is simple: the seafood must be fresh and cooked quickly to remain tender. Squid is often sold already cleaned, which saves a lot of preparation time. This healthful dish, loaded with tomatoes, fresh herbs, and low-fat fish, is a great option for nights when you're craving a light pasta dish.

4 tablespoons (2 fl oz/60 ml) olive oil

2 boneless, skinless salmon fillets, about 4 oz (125 g) each

Kosher salt and freshly ground pepper

2 large leeks, white and tender green parts only, sliced in half lengthwise and thinly sliced crosswise

2 cups (2 oz/60 g) arugula leaves, tough stems removed

8 oz (250 g) farfalle

2 tablespoons fresh lemon juice

SEARED SALMON WITH FARFALLE & LEEKS

HEALTHY NIGHT

Loaded with heart-healthy omega 3's, salmon adds pretty color and wonderful flavor to this pasta dish. If possible, seek out wild salmon over farmed for both health and environmental concerns. You can also substitute smoked salmon (just cut it up and add it at the end), which is readily available. This dish is also tasty served cold with a squeeze of lemon and a sprinkle of capers.

Warm 1 tablespoon of the olive oil in a large, nonstick frying pan over high heat. Season both sides of the salmon with salt and pepper. Place the salmon in the hot pan and cook, turning once, until nicely seared on the outside but still rare inside, about 3 minutes per side. Transfer to a plate, cover loosely with aluminum foil, and set aside.

Bring a large pot of generously salted water to a boil over high heat.

In a clean large frying pan, warm the remaining 3 tablespoons olive oil over medium-high heat. Add the leeks and season well with salt and pepper. Cook, stirring often, until soft and golden brown, about 8 minutes. Add the arugula and sauté until just wilted, about 3 minutes. Remove from the heat.

Meanwhile, add the farfalle to the boiling water and cook according to the package directions. Drain the pasta, reserving ½ cup (4 fl oz/125 ml) of the cooking water. Add the pasta to the frying pan with the leeks and arugula and place over medium heat. Stir in the lemon juice and reserved pasta-cooking water.

Flake the salmon into 1-inch (2.5-cm) pieces and gently fold it into the pasta, along with all the juices collected on the plate. Taste and adjust the seasoning and serve right away.

SERVES 4

Kosher salt and freshly ground pepper

12 oz (375 g) rigatoni

2 tablespoons olive oil

1 yellow onion, sliced

2 small heads radicchio (about ¾ lb/375 g total weight), cored, quartered and shredded

1 tablespoon chopped fresh rosemary

2 teaspoons balsamic vinegar

2 cups (16 fl oz/500 ml) whole milk

4 tablespoons (2 oz/60 g) unsalted butter

¼ cup (1½ oz/45 g) all-purpose flour

6 oz (180 g) Gorgonzola cheese, cut or broken into ½-inch (12-mm) pieces

⅓ cup (1½ oz/45 g) plain dried bread crumbs

BAKED RIGATONI WITH GORGONZOLA & RADICCHIO

Radicchio is a type of bitter red chicory, whose color and flavor mellows when it's sautéed. It's a delicious accompaniment with the salty richness of Gorgonzola. Round tubular shape of rigatoni works well for this dish, as the tubes become coated inside and out with the creamy cheese sauce. Serve with a side of Garlicky Roasted Mushrooms (page 116).

Bring a large pot of generously salted water to a boil over high heat. Add the rigatoni and cook according to the package directions. Drain well in a colander, rinse under cold water, and drain again. Transfer the pasta to a large bowl. Set aside.

Preheat the oven to 375°F (190°C).

Warm the olive oil in a large frying pan over high heat. Add the onion and sauté until translucent, about 4 minutes. Reduce the heat to low and season with salt and pepper. Cook, stirring occasionally, until the onion is golden brown, about 15 minutes. Add the radicchio, rosemary, and vinegar. Sauté until the radicchio is soft, about 5 minutes. Transfer to the bowl with the pasta.

In a small saucepan, warm the milk over low heat. In another saucepan, melt the butter over medium heat. Whisk the flour into the melted butter and continue whisking until it turns light brown, about 2 minutes. Slowly whisk in the warmed milk and bring to a very low simmer. Cook the sauce, stirring often, until it begins to thicken, about 2 minutes. Remove from the heat and season with salt and pepper.

Pour the white sauce over the pasta and toss to combine. Stir in the Gorgonzola. Taste and adjust the seasoning. Transfer the pasta to a 4-qt/4-l baking dish and sprinkle evenly with the bread crumbs.

Bake until the sauce is bubbling, and the cheese is melted, about 20 minutes. Let cool slightly and serve.

SERVES 6–8

Kosher salt and freshly ground pepper

½ lb (250 g) elbow macaroni

2 cups (16 fl oz/500 ml) whole milk

4 tablespoons (2 oz/60 g) unsalted butter

¼ cup (1½ oz/45 g) all-purpose flour

Freshly grated nutmeg

8 oz (250 g) sharp white Cheddar cheese, shredded (about 2 cups/8 oz/250 g)

4 oz (125 g) Gruyère cheese, shredded (about 1 cup/4 oz/125 g)

½ cup (2 oz/60 g) panko bread crumbs

CLASSIC MACARONI & CHEESE

OLD-FASHIONED GOODNESS

Once you discover how fast and delicious homemade macaroni and cheese is to make, you will never go back to boxed. The best part about it is that most of the ingredients are probably already in your pantry, and you can use just about any kind of shredded cheese you have on hand.

Preheat the oven to 375°F (190°C).

Bring a large pot of generously salted water to a boil over high heat. Add the macaroni and cook according to the package directions. Drain well in a colander, rinse under cold water, and drain again. Transfer the pasta to a large bowl. Set aside.

In a small saucepan, warm the milk over low heat. In another saucepan, melt the butter over medium heat. Whisk the flour into the melted butter and continue whisking until it turns light brown, about 2 minutes. Slowly whisk in the warmed milk and bring to a very low simmer. Cook the sauce, stirring often, until it begins to thicken, about 2 minutes. Remove from the heat and season with salt, pepper, and nutmeg.

Pour the white sauce over the pasta and stir to combine. Stir in the cheeses and season with salt and pepper. Transfer the macaroni and cheese to a 4-qt/4-l baking dish and sprinkle evenly with the bread crumbs.

Bake until hot throughout, the sauce is bubbling, and the bread crumbs are lightly browned, about 25 minutes. Let cool slightly and serve.

Mix up your routine with these delicious variations on the classic: See next page.

SERVES 6

SPINACH & MUSHROOM Warm 2 tablespoons olive oil in a frying pan over medium-high heat. Add 4 oz (125 g) sliced mushrooms, season with salt and pepper, and sauté until the mushrooms are browned and soft, about 4 minutes. Add 3 cups (3 oz) baby spinach leaves and sauté until just wilted, about 3 minutes. Add the contents of the pan to the bowl with the pasta and continue the recipe as directed.

MEXICAN MAC & CHEESE Substitute the cheeses with 2 cups (8 oz/250 g) shredded sharp Cheddar and 1 cup (4 oz/125 g) shredded pepper jack cheese. Stir in 3 tablespoons chopped fresh cilantro when you add the cheeses and continue with the recipe as directed. Omit the panko, and serve with fresh salsa and sliced avocado on the side.

SAUSAGE & RED PEPPER Warm 2 teaspoons olive oil in a frying pan over medium-high heat and add 8 oz (250 g) sweet or spicy Italian sausage, removed from its casing. Sauté the sausage, breaking up any clumps with your spoon, until cooked through, about 6 minutes. Add 1 seeded and chopped red bell pepper to the pan and sauté until the pepper is soft, about 4 minutes. Using a slotted spoon, transfer the sausage and peppers to the bowl with the pasta and continue with the recipe as directed.

BACON & CARAMELIZED ONION Cook 4 slices thick-cut bacon in a frying pan over medium-high heat until crisp, about 7 minutes. Transfer to paper towels to drain and, when cool enough to handle, tear into bite-sized pieces. Pour off and discard all but 1 tablespoon of the bacon grease from the pan and add 1 halved and sliced yellow onion. Raise the heat to high, season with salt and pepper, and sauté until translucent, about 4 minutes. Reduce the heat to low and sauté, still stirring often, until the onion turns deep brown in color, 25–30 minutes. Add the caramelized onion and torn bacon to the bowl with the pasta and continue with the recipe as directed.

MAC & CHEESE PARTY

For a fun dinner party idea, set up a make-your-own macaroni and cheese bar with all the variation ingredients at left. Let guests mix in their favorite cooked ingredients, have everyone add cheese sauce, and bake the separate, customized portions until bubbly.

Kosher salt and freshly ground pepper

8 oz (250 g) lasagna noodles

2 tablespoons olive oil, plus more for greasing

½ yellow onion, chopped

2 cloves garlic, minced

1 lb (500 g) ground beef

½ lb (250 g) sweet or spicy Italian sausage

2 cups (16 fl oz/500 ml) Marinara Sauce (page 16)

15 oz (470 g) whole-milk ricotta cheese

1 large egg, lightly beaten

12 oz (375 g) buffalo mozzarella cheese, thinly sliced

4 oz (125 g) low-moisture mozzarella cheese, shredded (about 1 cup)

3 tablespoons freshly grated Parmesan cheese

¼ cup (⅓ oz/10 g) lightly packed fresh basil leaves, chopped

BEEF & SAUSAGE LASAGNA WITH MARINARA

CROWD-PLEASER

There is no better meal for feeding a group than a lasagna. It can be made ahead of time, and even frozen a couple weeks in advance. Serve with a mixed green salad and Garlic Bread (page 111), and you are all set for a party!

Preheat the oven to 375°F (190°C).

Bring a large pot of generously salted water to a boil over high heat. Add the lasagna noodles and cook according to the package instructions. Drain well and lay the noodles in a single layer on an oiled baking sheet. Set aside.

Warm the olive oil in a frying pan over medium-high heat. Add the onion and sauté until translucent, about 5 minutes. Add the garlic and sauté just until soft, about 1 minute longer. Remove the sausage casings. Add the beef and sausage and cook, stirring occasionally and using your spoon to break up any clumps, until the meat is cooked through, about 10 minutes. Season with salt and pepper. Add the marinara sauce and stir to combine. Taste and adjust the seasoning. Set aside.

In a bowl, stir together the ricotta and egg and season well with salt and pepper. Set aside.

To assemble, coat a 9-by-13-inch (23-by-33-cm) baking dish with nonstick cooking spray and lay one-third of the noodles on the bottom. Top the noodle layer with half of the meat, half of the ricotta mixture (dollop it evenly), and one-third of the fresh mozzarella slices. Arrange another layer of noodles over the filling and top with the remaining meat, the remaining ricotta mixture, and about one-third of the remaining mozzarella slices. Place the final layer of noodles over all, scatter the remaining mozzarella slices and the shredded mozzarella on top, then sprinkle evenly with the Parmesan.

Bake until hot throughout and the sauce is bubbling, about 40 minutes. Let cool slightly, then top with the chopped basil, and serve.

SERVES 8–10

3 tablespoons olive oil

Kosher salt and freshly ground pepper

3 small eggplants, cut into chunks

¾ lb (375 g) ziti, penne, or other tubular pasta

2 cups (16 fl oz/500 ml) Bolognese Sauce (page 20)

2 Roma tomatoes, chopped

½ lb (250 g) fresh mozzarella cheese

¼ cup (¼ oz/7 g) loosely packed fresh basil leaves, sliced

¼ cup (1 oz/30 g) freshly grated Parmesan cheese

BAKED ZITI WITH EGGPLANT & BOLOGNESE

Preheat the oven to 450°F (230°C). Line 2 baking sheets with parchment paper or aluminum foil. In a small bowl, combine the oil and ½ teaspoon each salt and pepper. Drizzle the eggplant chunks with the oil mixture and arrange on the prepared sheets so they are not touching. Roast until golden, about 12–14 minutes. Remove from the oven, and let cool. Reduce the oven temperature to 375°F (190°C).

Meanwhile, bring a large pot of generously salted water to a boil over high heat. Add the ziti. Cook, stirring occasionally to prevent sticking, until still very al dente, about 2 minutes less than the package directions. Drain and rinse under running cold water to stop the cooking; drain well again.

Cut the mozzarella into small pieces. In a large bowl toss together the pasta, bolognese, roasted eggplant, tomatoes, mozzarella, and basil. Spread the pasta mixture on the bottom of a 9-by-12-by-12-by-2-inch (23-by-30-by-5-cm) or 1½ qt (1.5 l) baking dish. Sprinkle the pasta with the Parmesan. Cover with foil and bake for 20 minutes. Remove the foil and bake until the surface is golden and bubbly, about 5 minutes longer. Let cool for 10 minutes before serving.

SERVES 8–10

PLAN AHEAD

You can roast the eggplant up to 1 day in advance and store it in an airtight container or a resealable plastic bag in the refrigerator. Or, replace the eggplant with 2 small zucchini. Round out the meal with some Lemony Sautéed Kale with Garlic & Golden Raisins (page 118).

Kosher salt and freshly ground pepper

½ lb (500 g) jumbo shells

2 teaspoon olive oil, plus more for greasing

5 oz (155 g) arugula leaves, tough
stems removed

3 cups (24 oz/750 g) whole-milk ricotta cheese

6 tablespoons (1½ oz/45 g) freshly grated
Parmesan cheese

1 large egg, lightly beaten

1½ cups (12 fl oz/375 ml) Amatriciana Sauce
(page 17)

RICOTTA & ARUGULA STUFFED SHELLS WITH MEAT SAUCE

Bring a large pot of generously salted water to a boil over high heat. Add the pasta
shells and cook for about 2 minutes less than the package directions call for. Drain
well and arrange in a single layer on an oiled baking sheet. Set aside.

Preheat the oven to 375°F (190°C).

Warm the olive oil in a frying pan over medium-high heat. Add the arugula and sauté
until just wilted, about 3 minutes. Transfer to a cutting board and, when cool enough
to handle, chop finely. Set aside.

In a bowl, stir together the ricotta, 4 tablespoons (1 oz/30 g) of the Parmesan, and
the egg. Stir in the chopped arugula and season with salt and pepper.

Spread ¼ cup (2 fl oz/60 ml) of the amatriciana sauce on the bottom of a 9-by-13-inch
(23-by-33-cm) baking dish. Using a teaspoon, fill each shell with the ricotta mixture.
The shells should be full but not bursting open. Place each filled shell, open side up,
in the sauce in the baking dish. Cover the shells with the remaining 1¼ cups (10 fl oz/
315 ml) sauce and sprinkle evenly with the remaining 2 tablespoons Parmesan.

Cover the dish with aluminum foil and bake until the sauce is bubbling and the cheese
is melted, about 25 minutes. Let cool slightly and serve.

SERVES 4-6

Here, stuffed shells are enlivened
with the addition of savory and
colorful sautéed arugula. To make
this a vegetarian dish, switch the
pork-infused Amatriciana Sauce
to Arrabbiata Sauce (page 16),
Marinara Sauce (page 16), or
Pesto (page 21).

Kosher salt and freshly ground pepper

20 cannelloni tubes

2 tablespoons olive oil, plus more for greasing

1 yellow onion, chopped

2 cloves garlic, minced

1 lb (500 g) ground beef

2 cups (16 oz/500 g) whole-milk ricotta cheese

1½ tablespoons chopped fresh oregano

3 cups (24 fl oz/750 ml) Marinara Sauce (page 16)

½ cup (2 oz/60 g) shredded low-moisture mozzarella cheese

BEEF & OREGANO CANNELLONI

>>>>>>>>>

Here is another hearty, meaty dish for feeding a large group. You can mix up the meat with any combination of ground beef, pork, veal, turkey, chicken, or sausage. For a striking dinner party presentation, serve the cannelloni atop a bed of sautéed spinach with Tomato Bruschetta (page 106) on the side. Finish with a nice bottle of Chianti and dinner is served.

Bring a large pot of generously salted water to a boil over high heat. Cook 10 cannelloni at a time according to package directions, letting the water return to a boil between batches. Drain well and arrange in a single layer on an oiled baking sheet. When cool enough to handle, use a small knife to slit open each tube lengthwise. Set side.

Preheat the oven to 350°F (180°C).

Warm the olive oil in a frying pan over medium-high heat. Add the onion and sauté until translucent, about 5 minutes. Add the garlic and sauté just until soft, about 1 minute longer. Add the beef and season with salt and pepper. Cook, stirring occasionally and using your spoon to break up any clumps, until the meat is cooked through, about 10 minutes.

Transfer the beef to a large bowl and let cool for 10 minutes. Once the beef is cool, stir in the ricotta and oregano and season with salt and pepper.

Spread 1 cup (8 fl oz/250 ml) of the marinara sauce all over the bottom of a 9-by-13-inch (23-by-33-cm) baking dish. Fill each cannelloni tube with 1½ tablespoons of the beef mixture and place, seam side down, in the sauce in the baking dish. Cover the cannelloni with the remaining 2 cups (16 fl oz/500 ml) sauce and sprinkle evenly with the mozzarella.

Bake until hot throughout, the sauce is bubbling, and the cheese is lightly browned on top, about 25 minutes. Serve right away.

SERVES 8–10

Kosher salt and freshly ground pepper

1 lb (500 g) ziti

1 teaspoon olive oil

1 lb (500 g) sweet Italian sausage, casings removed

2 cups (16 fl oz/500 ml) Marinara Sauce (page 16)

6 oz (185 g) fresh mozzarella cheese, preferably buffalo, cut into ¾-inch (2-cm) cubes

¼ cup (⅓ oz/10 g) fresh basil leaves, chopped

4 oz (125 g) low-moisture mozzarella cheese, shredded (about 1 cup)

2 tablespoons freshly grated Parmesan cheese

BAKED ZITI WITH SWEET ITALIAN SAUSAGE

Preheat the oven to 350°F (180°C).

Bring a large pot of generously salted water to a boil over high heat. Add the ziti and cook according to the package directions. Drain well and transfer to a large bowl. Set aside.

Warm the olive oil in a frying pan over medium-high heat. Add the sausage and cook, stirring occasionally and using your spoon to break up any clumps, until cooked through, about 6 minutes. Using a slotted spoon, transfer the sausage to paper towels to drain.

Add the marinara sauce to the bowl with the pasta. Stir in the sausage, fresh mozzarella cubes, and basil and season well with salt and pepper. Transfer to a 4-qt/4-l baking dish and sprinkle evenly with the shredded mozzarella and the Parmesan.

Bake until the sauce is bubbling and the cheese is melted, 25–30 minutes. Let cool slightly and serve.

SERVES 8–10

You can use any shaped pasta (farfalle, rotelle, or shells to name a few) for this warm and comforting dish. If you want to add a vegetable to this recipe, try adding sautéed spinach, roasted red peppers, or sautéed mushrooms to the mix.

Kosher salt and freshly ground pepper

8 oz (250 g) lasagna noodles

3 tablespoons olive oil, plus 1 teaspoon and more for greasing

4 cloves garlic, minced

1 lb (500 g) white or brown mushrooms, brushed clean and sliced

10 oz (315 g) spinach leaves, tough stems removed

3 cups (24 oz/750 g) whole-milk ricotta cheese

1 large egg, lightly beaten

1 cup (8 fl oz/250 ml) Pesto (page 21)

8 oz (250 g) fontina cheese, shredded (about 2 cups/10 oz/300 g)

1 cup (8 fl oz/250 ml) Marinara Sauce (page 16)

MUSHROOM, SPINACH & PESTO LASAGNA WITH FONTINA CHEESE

FRESH IS BEST

>>>>>>>>

This is a really fresh and inspired vegetarian lasagna, featuring fresh spinach, both pesto and marinara sauces, and nutty, fontina cheese. This dish goes well with Tricolore Salad (see page 119).

Preheat the oven to 375°F (190°C).

Bring a large pot of generously salted water to a boil over high heat. Add the lasagna noodles and cook according to the package instructions. Drain well and lay the noodles in a single layer on an oiled baking sheet. Set aside.

Warm the 3 tablespoons olive oil in a frying pan over medium-high heat. Add the garlic and mushrooms, season well with salt and pepper, and cook, stirring often, until the mushrooms are golden brown and soft but still holding their shape, about 4 minutes. Transfer the mushroom mixture to a plate. Do not wipe the pan clean. In the same frying pan over medium-high heat, warm the 1 teaspoon olive oil. Add the spinach, season well with salt and pepper, and sauté until just wilted, about 3 minutes. Drain well and set aside.

In a bowl, stir together the ricotta and egg and season well with salt and pepper. Set aside. To assemble the lasagna, coat a 9-by-13-inch (23-by-33-cm) baking dish with nonstick cooking spray and lay one-third of the noodles on the bottom. Top the noodle layer with half of the ricotta mixture (dollop it evenly), all of the pesto, half of the mushrooms, half of the spinach, and one-third of the fontina. Arrange another layer of noodles over the filling and top with the remaining ricotta mixture, all of the marinara, the remaining mushrooms and spinach, and another one-third of the fontina. Place the final layer of noodles on top and scatter the remaining fontina evenly on top.

Bake until the sauce is bubbling, about 40 minutes. Let cool slightly and serve.

SERVES 8–10

Kosher salt and freshly ground pepper

20 manicotti tubes

5 carrots, peeled and cut into ¼-inch (6-mm) dice

⅓ cup (3 fl oz/80 ml) olive oil

2 cups (16 oz/500 g) whole-milk ricotta cheese

½ cup (2 oz/60 g) shredded low-moisture mozzarella cheese

2 tablespoons freshly grated pecorino cheese

1 large egg, lightly beaten

2 tablespoons chopped fresh basil

2 cups (16 fl oz/500 ml) whole milk

4 tablespoons (2 oz/60 g) unsalted butter

¼ cup (1½ oz/45 g) all-purpose flour

Freshly grated nutmeg

ROASTED CARROT & THREE-CHEESE MANICOTTI

Roasted carrots give this dish both a sweet and savory edge. You could also make this dish with half white sauce and half pesto for an herbal flavor. Serve this manicotti with Escarole Salad (page 109) for a wonderfully fresh and crisp accompaniment.

Bring a large pot of generously salted water to a boil over high heat. Cook 10 manicotti at a time according to the package directions, letting the water return to a boil between batches. Drain well and arrange in a single layer on an oiled baking sheet. When cool enough to handle, use a small knife to slit open each tube lengthwise. Set aside. Preheat the oven to 400°F (200°C).

Pile the carrots on a baking sheet lined with parchment paper. Drizzle with the olive oil, season well with salt and pepper, and toss to coat. Spread the carrots in an even layer on the pan and bake, stirring once about halfway through, until soft and caramelized, about 25 minutes. Let cool slightly, then transfer to a food processor. Add ¼ cup (2 oz/60 g) of the ricotta and process until smooth. Transfer to a large bowl. Stir in the remaining 1¾ cups (14 oz/440 g) ricotta, the mozzarella, pecorino, egg, and basil. Season with salt and pepper and set aside. Reduce the oven temperature to 350°F (180°C).

In a saucepan, warm the milk over low heat. In another saucepan, melt the butter over medium heat. Whisk the flour into the melted butter until it turns light brown, about 2 minutes. Slowly whisk in the milk and bring to a very low simmer. Cook the sauce, stirring often, until it begins to thicken, about 2 minutes. Remove from the heat and season with salt, pepper, and nutmeg. Spread ½ cup (4 fl oz/125 ml) of the white sauce all over the bottom of a 9-by-13-inch (23-by-33-cm) baking dish. Fill each manicotti tube with 1½ tablespoons of the carrot-ricotta mixture and place, seam side down, in the baking dish. Cover the manicotti with the remaining sauce. Bake until the sauce is bubbling and lightly browned, about 25 minutes. Let stand for 5 minutes, then serve.

SERVES 8–10

5 tablespoons (2½ oz/75 g) unsalted butter, plus more for the baking dish

2 tablespoons olive oil

1 lb (500 g) fresh cremini mushrooms, brushed cleaned, trimmed, and quartered

Kosher salt and freshly ground pepper

1 lb (500 g) short tubular pasta such as penne, ziti, or cavatappi

¼ cup (1½ oz/45 g) unbleached all-purpose flour

2 cups (16 fl oz/500 ml) milk, warmed

1 cup (8 fl oz/250 ml) crème fraîche

2½ cups (10 oz/315 g) shredded Comté

2 Roma tomatoes, sliced

½ cup (2 oz/60 g) panko bread crumbs or coarse dried bread crumbs

BAKED PENNE WITH COMTÉ & MUSHROOMS

Preheat the oven to 350°F (180°C). Lightly butter a shallow 9-by-13-inch (23-by-33-cm) baking dish. In a large frying pan over medium-high heat, warm the olive oil. Add the mushrooms and cook, stirring occasionally, until lightly browned, about 10 minutes. Season with salt and pepper, remove from the heat, and set aside.

Bring a large pot of generously salted water to a boil over high heat. Add the penne and cook according to the package instructions until the pasta is 1–2 minutes shy of being al dente. Drain the pasta in a colander, refresh under cold running water to prevent the pasta from sticking together, and drain again. Return the pasta pot to medium heat and add 4 tablespoons (2 oz/60 g) of the butter. When the butter has melted, whisk in the flour, reduce the heat to low, and cook and stir for 1 minute. Do not let the flour-and-butter paste brown. Gradually and carefully whisk in the warmed milk and then the crème fraîche, raise the heat to high, and continue to whisk until the mixture thickens, about 2 minutes. Turn off the heat.

Add the cheese a handful at a time, stirring after each addition until melted. Season with salt and pepper. Stir in the pasta and mushrooms. Transfer to the prepared baking dish and top with a single layer of tomato slices. Sprinkle evenly with the bread crumbs. Cut the remaining 1 tablespoon butter into tiny cubes, and dot the cubes over the bread crumbs. Bake until the surface is bubbling and the topping is crisp, about 25 minutes. Let stand for 5 minutes before serving.

SERVES 6–8

Think of this dish as French-style macaroni and cheese. Comté, a mild, nutty cheese, melts quickly into the warmed milk-crème fraîche mixture to form a sophisticated cheese sauce. Japanese-style bread crumbs, known as panko, form a crunchy crust.

SALADS & SIDES

About 20 cherry tomatoes,
or 2 large tomatoes

About 16 fresh basil leaves,
torn into small pieces

Flaked sea salt

8 slices coarse country bread,
about ½ inch (12 mm) thick

2 cloves garlic, peeled and left whole

¼ cup (2 fl oz/60 ml) extra-virgin olive oil

TOMATO BRUSCHETTA

The key to delicious tomato bruschetta is to use quality ingredients. If tomatoes are out of season, try sautéed broccoli rabe and garlic and top with olive oil and red pepper flakes. Or, see the notes on page 121 for using cherry tomatoes.

Prepare a charcoal or gas grill for direct grilling over medium-high heat, or preheat a broiler.

If using cherry tomatoes, stem them and cut them in half. If using large tomatoes, core and seed them and cut into ½-inch (12-mm) dice. In a bowl, combine the tomatoes, the basil, and a pinch of salt.

If grilling, using tongs, place the bread slices over the hottest part of the fire or directly over the heat elements and grill, turning once, until crisp and golden on both sides, about 3 minutes total.

If broiling, place the bread slices on a baking sheet and slip it under the broiler, about 4 inches (10 cm) from the heat source. Broil, turning once, until crisp and golden on both sides, about 3 minutes total.

Remove from the heat and immediately rub one side of each slice vigorously with a garlic clove, using 1 clove for 4 slices.

Arrange the bread slices, garlic side up, on a serving platter or divide among individual plates. Spoon the tomato mixture on the bread, dividing it evenly. Drizzle with the olive oil and serve right away.

SERVES 4

1 shallot, minced

1 tablespoon red wine vinegar

1 teaspoon Dijon mustard

2 tablespoons olive oil

Kosher salt and freshly ground pepper

1 head escarole, cored and chopped
(about 6 cups/6 oz/185 g)

1 small, crisp sweet-tart apple such as
Fuji or Honeycrisp, cored and thinly sliced

3 tablespoons walnut pieces, toasted

½ cup (3 oz/90 g) pitted and sliced
Medjool dates

3 oz (90 g) Manchego cheese, shaved

ESCAROLE SALAD WITH APPLE, WALNUTS, DATES & MANCHEGO

In a small bowl, stir together the shallot, vinegar, and mustard. Whisk in the olive oil
and season with salt and pepper. Set aside.

Put the escarole in a large bowl and toss with the dressing. Add the apple, walnuts, dates,
and cheese and toss to combine. Season with salt and pepper and serve right away.

SERVES 4-6

You can wash the escarole ahead
of time, dry very well, wrap
in paper towels, and store in
a locking plastic bag. Crunchy
walnuts, sweet and chewy dates,
tart apple slices, and salty
Manchego cheese create a full
array of textures and flavors
in this delicious and light salad.

2 Bosc pears, peeled, halved, and cored

1 tablespoon olive oil

1 teaspoon balsamic vinegar

Kosher salt and freshly ground pepper

1 tablespoon balsamic vinegar

1 teaspoon Dijon mustard

2 tablespoons olive oil

Salt and freshly ground pepper

1 head chicory, cored and chopped
(about 6 cups/6 oz/185 g)

4 oz (125 g) Stilton cheese, crumbled

2 tablespoons slivered almonds, toasted

CHICORY SALAD WITH ROASTED PEARS, STILTON & ALMONDS

Pears come to the market in fall and winter and are delicious when roasted. In the summertime you can substitute nectarines or peaches in this salad, which also provide a sweet contrast to the pungent blue cheese and toasted almonds. There are a couple ways to toast nuts: you can toast them in a dry skillet or put them on a baking sheet in a 350°F (180°C) oven. Either way, pay close attention as they burn very easily.

To make the pears: Preheat the oven to 375°F (190°C). In a bowl, toss the pear halves with the 1 tablespoon olive oil, 1 teaspoon vinegar, and season with salt and pepper. Arrange them, cut side up, in a baking dish. Bake for 25 minutes. Flip the pears over, baste with the pan juices, and bake until golden brown and fork-tender, about 25 minutes longer. Once cool enough to handle, cut each pear half lengthwise into 4 slices. Set aside.

In a small bowl, stir together the 1 tablespoon vinegar and mustard. Whisk in the 2 tablespoons olive oil and season with salt and pepper. Put the chicory in a large bowl and toss with the dressing. Divide the dressed greens among plates. Garnish with the pear slices, crumbled cheese, and slivered almonds. Serve right away.

SERVES 4–6

3 tablespoons butter

3 tablespoons olive oil

3 large cloves garlic, minced

2 tablespoons chopped fresh flat-leaf parsley

1 loaf ciabatta or other rustic bread

Kosher salt and freshly ground pepper

GARLIC BREAD

Preheat the oven to 350°F (180°C).

Melt the butter and olive oil in a small frying pan over medium heat. Add the garlic and cook just until it softens, about 1 minute. Remove the pan from the heat and stir in the parsley. Cut the ciabatta in half lengthwise. Using a pastry brush, cover both of the cut sides of the bread with the melted butter mixture and season generously with salt and pepper. Put the bread back together so that the buttered sides of the bread are facing each other. Wrap tightly in aluminum foil and place in the oven until warmed through, about 10 minutes.

Carefully remove the foil, slice, and serve right away.

SERVES 4-6

Crisp garlic bread, flecked with fresh parsley, is the perfect accompaniment to saucy pasta dishes. Leftovers can be cut into cubes and used as garlic croutons on salads. For bread crumbs, leave leftover garlic bread on the counter to dry overnight, then blend into crumbs in a food processor, and add to pasta dishes.

WHAT YOU NEED

1 lb (500 g) brussels sprouts, quartered

3 tablespoons olive oil, plus more as needed

2 tablespoons honey

1 tablespoon balsamic vinegar

1½ tablespoons chopped fresh rosemary

Kosher salt and freshly ground black pepper

2 tablespoons hazelnuts

BRUSSELS SPROUTS WITH HONEY, ROSEMARY & HAZELNUTS

CARAMELIZED FLAVOR

The result of tossing Brussel sprouts in honey, olive oil, vinegar, and fresh rosemary before a quick stint in the oven? Tender, caramelized, deeply scented, and crispy vegetables that even picky eaters can't resist. This recipe is also delicious with winter squash.

Preheat the oven to 400°F (200°C).

In a large bowl, toss the brussels sprouts with the 3 tablespoons olive oil, the honey, the vinegar, and the rosemary. Season generously with salt and pepper. Transfer to a baking sheet lined with parchment paper and spread in a single layer. Roast, stirring once about halfway through, until fork-tender and caramelized, about 25 minutes. If the sprouts seem dry when you stir them, drizzle with another tablespoon or more of olive oil.

In a small, dry nonstick frying pan over medium heat, toast the hazelnuts, shaking the pan a few times, until very aromatic, about 3 minutes. Pour immediately onto a cutting board, let cool slightly, and chop coarsely.

Transfer the Brussels sprouts to a serving dish and toss with the hazelnuts. Season with salt and pepper and serve right away.

SERVES 4

3 *each* small red and yellow beets

2 tablespoons olive oil

Kosher salt and freshly ground pepper

3 oranges

1 bulb fennel

3 tablespoons fresh orange juice

1 large shallot, minced

1 tablespoon Champagne or
white wine vinegar

1 teaspoon Dijon mustard

Kosher salt and freshly ground pepper

3 tablespoons extra-virgin olive oil

2 cups (2 oz/60 g) watercress leaves

ROASTED BEET, FENNEL, ORANGE & WATERCRESS SALAD

Preheat the oven to 400°F (200°C).

Trim, peel, and quarter the beets. Pile all the beets on a baking sheet lined with parchment paper. Drizzle with the olive oil, season well with salt and pepper, and toss to coat. Spread the beets in a single layer and roast, stirring a few times, until fork-tender, 40–50 minutes. Remove from the oven and set aside.

While the beets are roasting, section the oranges: Working over a bowl with 1 orange at time and using a very sharp paring knife, pare away the peels and pith. Carefully cut between the membranes of the orange to release each orange section. Let the sections and the juice fall into the bowl as you work. When you have cut out each section, squeeze any remaining juice from the membrane into the bowl.

Remove and discard the feathery fronds of the fennel. Quarter, core, and slice the fennel.

To make the vinaigrette, strain the orange juice into a large salad bowl. Add the shallot, vinegar, mustard, and season with salt and pepper. Pour in the olive oil slowly, whisking until well blended. Taste and adjust the seasoning.

To assemble the salad, add the warm beets, orange sections, fennel, and watercress to the bowl with the dressing. Toss to coat all the ingredients well with the vinaigrette. Adjust the seasoning again, if needed. Serve right away.

SERVES 4

A FESTIVE BOWL

The watercress adds a peppery bite to this juicy salad, which is ideal for entertaining. You could also add goat cheese or nuts to the mix for a hit of protein or crunch. Serve this salad with a seafood pasta dish, such as Seared Salmon with Farfalle & Leeks (page 84).

1 lb (500 g) white or brown mushrooms, brushed clean and quartered

3 tablespoons olive oil

1 tablespoon sherry vinegar

4 cloves garlic, minced

Kosher salt and freshly ground pepper

2 tablespoons chopped fresh flat-leaf parsley

GARLICKY ROASTED MUSHROOMS

>>>>>>>>>>

Just a few simple ingredients and some time in a very hot oven make this a very flavorful side dish that can also work as a rustic sauce on top of grilled steaks. You can use any kind of mushrooms you have on hand. For a variation, add 1 tablespoon capers. Or stir in a couple tablespoons of crème fraîche and use to top over egg noodles.

Preheat the oven to 450°F (230°C).

In a bowl, toss the mushrooms with the olive oil, vinegar, and garlic. Season well with salt and pepper. Transfer to a baking sheet and spread in a single layer.

Roast the mushrooms, stirring once about halfway through, until fork-tender and dark brown, about 25 minutes. Stir in the parsley and serve right away.

SERVES 4

2 tablespoons olive oil

¼ cup (1½ oz/45 g) chopped onion

3 cloves garlic, minced

1½ lb (750 g) kale, stemmed and chopped

Kosher salt and freshly ground pepper

½ cup (4 fl oz/125 ml) low-sodium chicken or vegetable broth

2 tablespoons golden raisins

Juice of ½ lemon

LEMONY SAUTÉED KALE WITH GARLIC & GOLDEN RAISINS

Braising greens with chicken broth is a great way to add big flavor. You can substitute any greens in this recipe including spinach and chard. Golden raisins add a sweet and chewy surprise. Try substituting dried cherries or cranberries for a tangy note. Pair this dish with something meaty, such as Beef & Sausage Lasagna with Marinara (page 94), to balance out the richness.

Warm the olive oil in a large frying pan over medium-high heat. Add the onion and sauté until translucent, about 5 minutes. Add the garlic and sauté just until soft, about 1 minute longer.

Add the kale and season well with salt and pepper. Toss to coat the kale evenly with the oil and sauté, stirring occasionally, until all of the kale is wilted, about 3 minutes. Add the chicken broth and the raisins and cook until the liquid is mostly absorbed, about 5 minutes.

Remove from the heat and stir in the lemon juice. Taste and adjust the seasoning. Serve right away.

SERVES 4

3 tablespoons olive oil

2 tablespoons fresh lemon juice

Kosher salt and freshly ground pepper

1 head radicchio, cored and separated into leaves (about 1½ cups/1½ oz/45 g)

2 cups (2 oz/60 g) baby arugula

2 cups (3 oz/90 g) chopped romaine lettuce

1 can (15 oz/470 g) hearts of palm, drained and sliced

2 oz (60 g) Parmesan cheese, shaved

TRICOLORE SALAD WITH HEARTS OF PALM & PARMESAN

In a small bowl, whisk together the olive oil and lemon juice. Season with salt and pepper. Set aside.

Tear the radicchio leaves into bite-sized pieces. In a large bowl, combine the radicchio, arugula, and romaine lettuces. Pour in the dressing and toss to coat each lettuce leaf. Stir in the hearts of palm and garnish with the shaved Parmesan. Serve right away.

SERVES 4-6

Red, yellow, and green lettuce leaves come together for a pretty presentation and with a variety of flavors from bitter to sweet. Eat this salad alongside Cavatappi with Pesto, Potatoes & Green Beans (page 45), with a glass of crisp white wine, al fresco.

6 small sweet, red tomatoes such as Roma or Campari (about 1¼ lb/625 g total weight)

2 red bell peppers

1 tablespoon unsalted butter

4 tablespoons (2 fl oz/60 ml) olive oil

3 thick slices (about 1 inch/2.5 cm) sourdough bread, cut into ½-inch (12-mm) cubes

Kosher salt and freshly ground pepper

1 shallot, chopped

2 teaspoons red wine vinegar

2 tablespoons chopped fresh basil

ROASTED RED PEPPER, TOMATO & SOURDOUGH CROUTON SALAD

Cut the tomatoes into ½-inch (12-mm) pieces and put in a large nonreactive bowl.

Using tongs or a large fork, hold 1 pepper at a time directly over the flame of a gas burner, or place directly on the grate. Roast, turning as needed, until blistered and charred black on all sides, 10–15 minutes total. (Alternatively, place the peppers under a preheated broiler, as close as possible to the heating element, and roast to char them on all sides, turning as needed.) Transfer the peppers to a bowl, cover with plastic wrap or a clean kitchen towel, and set aside to steam until cooled, about 20 minutes. Once cool, peel or rub away the charred skins, then seed and chop the peppers. Add to the bowl with the tomatoes.

In a nonstick frying pan over high heat, melt the butter in 2 tablespoons of the olive oil. Add the cubed sourdough and season well with salt and pepper. Toast the bread, stirring only occasionally so that each side has time to brown, until nice and golden on all sides, about 5 minutes total. Add the croutons to the bowl with the tomatoes and peppers.

In a small bowl, stir together the shallot and vinegar. Whisk in the remaining 2 tablespoons olive oil and season with salt and pepper. Pour the dressing over the tomatoes, peppers, and croutons and toss to coat well. Stir in the basil, then taste and adjust the seasoning. Serve right away.

SERVES 4-6

A riff on a panzanella, this pretty salad is a nice accompaniment to a warm bowl of pasta. Store tomatoes at room temperature, not in the refrigerator, since cold temperatures turn tomatoes mushy and mealy. If it isn't tomato season, choose cherry tomatoes (about 1¼ lb/625 g, halved), which tend to be flavorful all year round and make a great substitution in this salad.

MENUS

From busy weeknights with kids to entertaining guests on a Saturday, planning a delicious, balanced dinner is a cinch with these menus as your guide. For shortcuts on a busy night, see page 13.

MANIC MONDAY

Pull out the pre-made frozen sauce, meatballs, and bread to thaw on Sunday for an effortless homemade dinner on Monday.

PENNETTE WITH MINI MEATBALLS (page 62)
LEMONY SAUTÉED KALE (page 118)
GARLIC BREAD (page 111)
FOR THE ADULTS Red wine
FOR THE KIDS Shirley Temples

HEALTHY & HEARTY

Pasta night gets a healthy makeover with the addition of nutritious vegetable mix-ins and a hearty side salad.

PENNETTE WITH KALE & FETA (page 42)
GARLICKY ROASTED MUSHROOMS (page 116)
BRUSSELS SPROUTS WITH HONEY (page 112)
FOR THE KIDS & ADULTS Seltzer with lemons and limes

ROMANTIC NIGHT-IN

An elegant pasta dish and your favorite cocktail is just the ticket for date night.

SLOW-COOKED PORK & FENNEL RAGÙ (page 59)
TRICOLORE SALAD (page 119)
FOR THE ADULTS Your favorite cocktail

KIDS RULE

Little hands are perfect for picking basil leaves from their stems. Have an adult assist as they whirl the pesto in a blender.

1 RECIPE PESTO (PAGE 21), MIXED WITH YOUR FAVORITE COOKED PASTA SHAPE
TOMATO BRUSCHETTA (page 106)
FOR THE ADULTS Crisp white wine
FOR THE KIDS Sparkling lemonade

COMFORT FOOD FEAST

Lasagna is perhaps the most comforting pasta dish of all. Warm up to this meal on a chilly night, with a side of garlic bread.

BEEF & SAUSAGE LASAGNA WITH MARINARA (page 94)
ROASTED BEET SALAD (page 115)
FOR THE ADULTS Red wine
FOR THE KIDS Root beer soda

SEAFOOD SUPPER

Satisfy seafood cravings with these simple dishes. Serve the two sauces with a big bowl of unsauced linguine, buffet-style.

LINGUINE WITH CLAMS (page 77)
LINGUINE WITH SPICY CALAMARI (page 83)
FOR THE ADULTS Your favorite wine
FOR THE KIDS Sparkling apple juice

INDEX

weldon**owen**

1045 Sansome Street, Suite 100, San Francisco, CA 94111

www.weldonowen.com

PASTA NIGHT

Conceived and produced by Weldon Owen, Inc.
In collaboration with Williams-Sonoma, Inc.
3230 Van Ness Avenue, San Francisco, CA 94109

A WELDON OWEN PRODUCTION

Copyright © 2014 Weldon Owen, Inc.
and Williams-Sonoma, Inc.

Printed and bound in China by 1010 Printing, Ltd.

First printed in 2014

10 9 8 7 6 5

Library of Congress Control Number: 2014938648

ISBN 13: 978-1-61628-797-9
ISBN 10: 1-61628-797-7

Weldon Owen is a division of

BONNIER

WELDON OWEN, INC

President & Publisher Roger Shaw
SVP, Sales & Marketing Amy Kaneko
Finance Manager Philip Paulick

Associate Publisher Amy Marr
Associate Editor Emma Rudolph

Creative Director Kelly Booth
Art Director Ashley Lima
Senior Production Designer Rachel Lopez Metzger

Production Director Chris Hemesath
Associate Production Director Michelle Duggan

Photographer Erin Kunkel
Food Stylist Erin Quon
Prop Stylist Leigh Noe

ACKNOWLEDGEMENTS

Weldon Owen wishes to thank the following people for
their generous support in producing this book:
David Bornfriend, Marisa Kwek, Chuck Luter, Eve Lynch,
Lori Nunokawa, Elizabeth Parson, and Sharon Silva